T0127424

A
REPLACEMENT *for*

RELIGION

A
REPLACEMENT
for

RELIGION

The School of Life

Published in 2019 by The School of Life
First published in the USA in 2020
70 Marchmont Street, London WC1N 1AB
Copyright © The School of Life 2019
Designed and typeset by Marcia Mihotich
Printed in Latvia by Livonia

A proportion of this book has appeared online at
www.theschooloflife.com/thebookoflife

Every effort has been made to contact the copyright holders of the
material reproduced in this book. If any have been inadvertently
overlooked, the publisher will be pleased to make restitution at
the earliest opportunity.

The School of Life is a resource for helping us understand
ourselves, for improving our relationships, our careers and our
social lives – as well as for helping us find calm and get more
out of our leisure hours. We do this through creating films,
workshops, books and gifts.

www.theschooloflife.com

ISBN 978-1-912891-03-0

10 9 8 7 6 5 4 3 2

CONTENTS

I.

INTRODUCTION:

THE DEATH OF GOD

✳

For a great many people, in large parts of the world, it has gradually become impossible to believe in anything divine. However consoling and uplifting it might be to have faith, there are simply too many rational arguments that stand in the way of being able to trust in stories of powerful, benevolent deities who have our interests at heart and will ensure our ultimate redemption. As Friedrich Nietzsche tersely – and legendarily – put it: 'God is dead. God remains dead. And we have killed him.' (The Gay Science, 1882).

The standard atheist view is that this is the end of the story. Once belief has been dismissed, and God's existence proved impossible, everything about religions should henceforth be ignored and disappear. The door can be closed on millennia of belief in what is, when viewed without sentiment, mere hocus pocus.

However, this view neglects how much of religion has never been about belief. A great deal of the practical activity and psychological insight of religion has been independent of prayer, levitating angels and supernatural incidents. Religions have put on communal gatherings, helped us with relationships, marked out the seasons, written ethical codes, buried us, celebrated births and rites of passage, tried to encourage kind and forgiving behaviour, built sublime gathering places, connected us to nature, commissioned works of art and organised meals, periods of fasting and pilgrimages. In other words, alongside spiritual redemption, religions have been interested in our ethical and emotional wellbeing as well.

When belief first went into decline in north-western Europe in the middle of the nineteenth century, many commentators wondered where humanity would – in an increasingly secular future – find the kind of guidance that religions had once provided. Where would ethical counsel come from? How would self-understanding be achieved? What would determine our sense of purpose? To whom would we turn in despair? Where would we gather for a feeling of belonging?

One answer – hesitantly and then increasingly boldly articulated – came to the fore: culture. *Culture could replace scripture.* There was, it was proposed by certain theorists, a convincing set of substitutes for the teachings of the faiths within the canon of culture. The plays of Sophocles and Racine, the paintings of Botticelli and Rembrandt, the literature of Goethe and Baudelaire, the philosophy of Plato and Schopenhauer, the musical compositions of Liszt and Wagner, the architecture of Palladio and Wren: these would provide the raw materials from which an adequate replacement for the assistance and consolations of the faiths could be formulated.

With this idea in mind, an unparalleled investment in culture followed in many decreasingly faithful nations. Vast numbers of libraries, concert halls, university humanities departments and museums were constructed around the world with the conscious intention of filling the chasm that religion had once occupied. Lest we miss the point, the designers of the British Library's new reading room specified that its vast central dome should have precisely the same circumference as St Peter's in Rome.

Culture will replace scripture.

When commissioning its new national museum, the Netherlands entrusted the task to the foremost church architect of the day, Pierre Cuypers, whose Rijksmuseum was indistinguishable from a home for worship. Museums were – as the rallying crying put it – to be our new cathedrals.

The cathedrals of secularism.

That culture might replace scripture remains an intriguing and compelling concept. And yet it has, to all intents and purposes, been entirely ignored. Culture has *not* in any way replaced scripture. Our museums are not our new cathedrals. They are smart filing cabinets for the art of the past. Our libraries are not our homes for the soul. They are architectural encyclopaedias. And if we were to show up at any university humanities' department in urgent search of purpose and meaning, or break down in a museum gallery in a quest for forgiveness or charity, we would be swiftly removed. The intensity of need and emotional craving that religions once willingly engaged with have not been thought acceptable within the contemporary cultural realm. The implication is that any moderately educated and sensible person already knows how to manage the business of living and dying well enough. Those who have produced culture may have sought to transform and inspire us; those who guard and interpret it have restricted themselves to a sober and curatorial interpretation of its function. No wonder we may still be casting around for ways to arrange our minds in the wake of religion's ebb.

The faiths may have gone away, but the emotional needs which led us to invent them remain highly active within us, still seeking urgent care and resolution. No less than our ancestors, we crave to learn to live and die well, to connect with others, to atone for our faults, to find redemption for our mistakes, to mark the passage of time and to be uplifted and consoled. Much that is in religion is intermittently too wise and too useful to be restricted merely to those who happen to believe in it.

The proposed way forward is not to dismiss religion altogether, *it is to strive* (as this book will attempt to show) *to replace it*. This replacement has nothing to do with updating the supernatural or obedience-based aspects of religion. The effort proceeds, in a spirit of radical modesty, in the opposite direction: towards a close understanding of what religions were able to offer us *outside of the supernatural, in the aesthetic and psychological spheres*, with a view to making some of this available, in an updated and digestible form, for our own times.

Within the project of replacing religion, The School of Life has been both inspired and cautioned by the example of a man who attempted just this: the French sociologist Auguste Comte (1798–1857). Comte began with a familiar and sensible starting point: an awareness that religions had ceased to be believable to most people, but that aspects of them continued to offer us a great deal. His idea was to mine religion in general, and Catholicism in particular, for ideas and resources in order to launch a new ideological movement that he termed 'a religion for humanity.'

Comte's replacement religion was a mixture of the charming, the useful and the unfortunately (though not necessarily fairly) easy-to-ridicule. In two volumes outlining its contents called the *Summary Exposition of the Universal Religion*, Comte announced that the new secular religion would have twelve updated 'saints', no longer supernatural heroes and heroines, but great figures from politics, science and the arts (Descartes, Goethe and

Voltaire among them). Every month of the year would be dedicated to one of these, with members attending lectures and reading groups and memorising passages of their work.

Auguste Comte, inventor of a Religion for Humanity.

Comte understood how much emotional guidance had been offered by religions and imagined a network of modernised priests, who would not try to save souls but would dispense useful advice on challenges like marriage, bringing up children, coping with illness and facing up to mortality. There would also be lectures and seminars offered on the key topics of emotional life.

As a former Catholic, Comte appreciated how much religions owed their impact to art and architecture. He envisaged a network of 'temples to humanity', highly attractive community centres, drawing on the talents of the best builders and painters of the day, which would provide a focal point where adherents could gather every week and listen to talks and kindle their friendships. Comte specified that above the west-facing stage, there should be a sentence written in gold letters capturing the essence of his new philosophy: '*Connais toi pour t'amtéliorer*' – 'Know yourself to improve yourself'.

Comte's plans were a mixed success. Though the press of the day mocked him as an eccentric and worse, a devoted core rallied to the cause. Brazil, then a young country, was particularly interested in his programme and a number of temples to humanity were built in four Brazilian cities, hosting classes, secular sermons and celebrations of the lives of non-religious 'saints' like Montaigne or Galileo. The temples survive to this day.

Temple to Humanity, Porto Alegre, Brazil.

But some of Comte's plans had more unfortunate sides. The 'religion for humanity' was at points redolent of a cult – that is, a community irrationally devoted to its leader – a fateful move for an ideology meant to attract people who had presumably had more than enough of worship or veneration. Against considerable opposition from his acolytes, Comte insisted that his girlfriend Clotilde should be venerated in every temple as the symbol of feminine wisdom, a touching gesture but strategically unwise.

Clotilde de Vaux, Comte's girlfriend.

And Comte couldn't resist moves that suggested that his community might be unreasonably focused on him. His modernised priests were meant to wear white tunics and a chain around their necks bearing Comte's image on one side and Plato's on the other. Their talks were to end with a little homily to Comte: 'Great teacher and Master, revealer of Humanity, prophet of the future, founder of the one universal religion.' It was no wonder that things didn't properly take off.

Whatever its shortcomings, Comte's 'religion for humanity' was a highly suggestive and thought-inducing experiment. It accurately zeroed in on the need to provide a replacement for some of the activities and concepts that had accompanied religions for most of human history – and sought to reimagine them for a secular world. It was a creative attempt to rescue some of what is beautiful, touching, reasonable and wise from what no longer seems true.

This book is an attempt by The School of Life to find – in our own way – a replacement for religion. This is not an attempt to start a cult (we don't care for worship, medals of founders, or portraits of our partners). We want to look at those aspects of the modern world that seem to be going badly and where problems can, in our view, specifically be traced back to the disappearance of ideas found within religion and the process of bad secularisation that followed its decline. Importantly, though our ambitions are stated in a book, they are not limited to a book. This is a deeply practical project with the aim of working a tangible impact. We want to suggest a range of interventions, drawn from philosophy, psychotherapy, art, architecture and the non-supernatural aspects of religion, that aims to make the business of living and dying well ever so slightly easier, as well as less lonely and confusing.

✳

II

THE ILLS OF MODERNITY

✳

We situate the need for a replacement for religion in a variety of psychological and emotional problems (unwittingly and unknowingly) generated for us by secular life. The conditions of modernity are in many ways profoundly better than those under which the vast majority of humanity lived for more or less the whole of history. But, along with its manifest benefits, modernity has brought a special range of troubles into our lives which we would be wise to try to unpick and understand.

Without as yet pushing in detail for what the solutions might be, we identify eight central ills stemming from certain ideals of modern life, to which any replacement for religion would have to locate responses.

I. PERFECTIBILITY

A fundamental tenet of modern societies is that perfection is within our grasp. Science, that most prized of contemporary tools, seems to guarantee us that we will, eventually, be able to overcome all that bedevils us: the pain, stupidity and error which make us so much less than we might be. It is simply a matter of time.

Our societies stress that it is within our capacities – individually and collectively – to aim for perfection. The modern era was founded upon astonishing achievements and improvements across almost every field of endeavour: we learnt to heat our houses, to feed and clothe ourselves adequately, to criss-cross the globe, to defeat disease and to introduce reliable mechanisms for learning, law and justice.

Our many improvements have imbued us with an unparalleled confidence, resulting in a notion that progress is a preordained and general rule of existence. We know that we may, of course, right now, be facing considerable challenges and reversals and that there is much evidence of our ongoing proclivity for stubbornness and stupidity. But we refuse to hold our sorrows as inevitable: rather, they are a sign of interrupted and delayed progress. Even death may one day be solved.

A problematic result of this grand vision of human progress is that our ongoing imperfections weigh upon us all the more heavily: we are prone, more than our forebears, to feel profoundly frustrated, impatient, cursed and betrayed with all that continues to defy our will.

We respond to political or economic stagnation with rage at the stupidity of those who lead us; we are unwilling to countenance (as our ancestors once did) the fact that human societies are hugely complex machines. The unhappiness of relationships is quickly ascribed to being with the wrong person – as opposed to the result of the inherently arduous goal of trying to be happy in multiple dimensions with another person over a lifetime. We are no less ambitious around our labour. We look askance at the previous, routine assumption that our jobs would always, in some ways, be something of a curse: we no longer work merely for money, we work to fulfil our souls. As for our psyches, we believe ourselves capable of overcoming any confusion or compulsions generated in our childhoods and of mastering our minds through the insights of therapy.

For most of history, we lived with a degree of reconciliation to the idea of ongoing woe and turmoil. With modernity was born the beautiful and fateful notion that this world could, through the application of intelligence, be rendered conclusively saner, more manageable and kinder. The origins of this attitude were immensely noble but the results have been strange and unexpected. We have too often come to despise and lament the actual conditions of our lives.

II. OPTIMISM

Modern societies are profoundly optimistic in temperament. They imply that our manner should be upbeat, our spirits high and our greetings enthusiastic. Expecting things to go well is presented as the best way to ensure that they will, in fact, do so. And presenting a cheerful front to others is assumed to be a reliable method for getting them to like us and to build up sincere bonds with strangers.

But our optimism has been a curse. When sunny expectations meet with an obstacle, they are readier to flip to its opposite, anger. Betrayed hope places us at greater risk of nitpicking, sulking, irritation and rage. What these behaviours have in common is insulted optimism: they are the legacy of a feeling that things were meant to be so much better than they have turned out. We are shocked and offended by the stupidity of others, the failings of institutions, the greed and selfishness that circulate and the prevalence of what feel like unwarranted errors. We are outraged by the immemorial condition of the world, our lives consumed by a disappointment fermented by what began as the sweetest of outlooks.

These dangers aside, we are pushed to imagine that being optimistic will make us more attractive to others; but oddly a determinedly jolly and upbeat outlook can in fact cut us off from communion with those around us, for our most profound reality is that we all have deep zones of worry, regret, inadequacy and shame that we long to see reflected in others and cannot when the mood must be sunny. It is the confession of darkness that allows us to get genuinely close to another person – just as it is insistent optimism that will, unexpectedly, reinforce us in our loneliness.

III. INDIVIDUALISM

For most of history, all that was felt to be required to understand a person's identity was a set of facts that had pretty been much settled at the moment of birth: one was defined by one's gender, by the social rank of one's parents, by the geographical zone one was born in and by the religious sect one's family belonged to.

But in the second half of the 18th century, a new ideology began that set its face against all accidents of birth and beckoned us to fashion ourselves in our own style across our lives, a hopeful, dynamic philosophy known today as individualism.

When we meet a stranger, we do not, as in the past, ask them about their ancestors, their religion or the place they grew up in. We ask them, first and foremost, what they 'do', for it is our work that has, more than anything else, come to be seen as the crucible of our individuality.

However, the connection between work and selfhood has ushered in distinctive new problems, for a work-based identity is by its nature extremely unstable: we are a sacking, a profit downgrade or a retirement away from losing an established sense of self. Equally, we may be transformed by a promotion, a newspaper profile or a flotation. Our identities are caught in a turbulent oscillation between hope and fear.

Our job-oriented identity is further buffeted by the constant presence of competition in a market economy: our status depends on victories over others. We can become impressive only if others fail. And if they succeed, our own attainments lose their lustre. We end up wanting others to sink because, every time they do so, our own prestige will be enhanced. Without any intentional malice, we have constructed a world of continuous psychological, as well as economic, rivalry.

An individualistic philosophy centred on careers means that what we do outside of paid work comes to seem negligible or irrelevant. Our efforts with our families, our friendships, our enthusiasms don't count in the eyes of others as any real answer to the question of 'what we do' because these pursuits are disconnected from a salary – and so must in turn grow diminished in our own eyes. There is a harsh irony: individualism was supposed to highlight our unique, intimate character, but it has, in practice, sharply reduced our sense of who we might be.

It is not surprising that the first great sociologist to investigate suicide – Émile Durkheim – discovered that the more individualistic a society becomes, the more the rate of suicide rises. It is not poverty or illness as such that drive us to the ultimate act of despair, it is the sense that who we are has no meaning outside of visible success in the realm of work.

IV. EXCEPTIONALISM

Modern societies continually stress that it is within our power to achieve a mighty destiny. Whatever the initial hurdles, we can, so the suggestion goes, overcome them all through hard work and the exercise of our will – thereby forging an exemplary and extraordinary path. We may reach other planets, amass fortunes, run the country, make stunning discoveries in science or produce an outstanding film or novel. We do not have to adhere to that most dispiriting of epithets: ordinary. We can, through our effort and brilliance, escape the herd.

This emphasis on heroism is meant to be encouraging. We are asked to feel that we too could – whatever obstacles we face – astound the world.

This belief in the potential of all has a deeply generous origin, but its effect is profoundly punitive, because we are inevitably destined to be very ordinary in most aspects of our lives. By necessity almost all of us will aggregate around the average, an unheroic truth emphasised by a central image of statistical analysis, the bell curve.

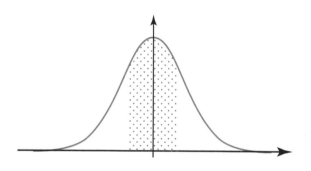

The majority of us will occupy this space – the middle ground.

Most of us will have close-to-average incomes, close-to-average relationships, more-or-less-average looks and deeply average talents. In any aspect of life, in any quality or endeavour, only a fraction of the population can ever stand out.

But even though we are destined to be ordinary, we live in a culture that ardently neglects or disparages this basic truth. It emphasises the likelihood of satisfying marriages, though ninety five percent of unions are merely tolerable compromises; it speaks of great jobs, though ninety-five percent of employment will be significantly compromised; and it valorises fame, though there are hardly any famous people (let alone contented famous ones). Our sights are set on deeply improbable objectives. It feels cruel to rule them out, but it may in reality be even crueller to incite them.

As a result of a generously intended idea, we end up despising the actual conditions of our lives, hate ourselves for not having done more, bitterly envy those who have triumphed and neglect to appreciate the qualities of what and who is actually to hand.

V. MERITOCRACY

Our societies firmly believe in the concept of meritocracy, that is, the faith that we should be free to make a success of our lives if we have sufficient talent and energy and that there should be no obstacles to our efforts based on class, gender or race.

All voices on the political spectrum are committed to an ideology which states that the highest form of political justice is a nation where the talented can rise whatever their backgrounds. A good society has become synonymous with a meritocratic one.

However, this very well-meaning idea carries with it some rather less appealing implications, for if we are to believe that those at the top truly deserve their success, then those at the bottom must surely truly deserve their failure. Under the aegis of a meritocratic worldview, an element of justice enters into the distribution of penalties as well as rewards. We move from thinking of the poor as 'unfortunates' – deserving of compassion and kindness – to thinking of them as something far harsher: 'losers'.

A society that thinks of itself as meritocratic converts poverty from a condition of honourable, if painful, bad luck into evidence of personal incompetence. The burden of failure rises exponentially.

VI. ANTHROPOCENTRISM

The modern age is inherently anthropocentric in outlook (from *anthropos*, Greek for human), that is, it places human beings and their experience and concerns at the centre of the hierarchy, above the claims of nature, animals, gods or the universe more broadly. We are now, in every way, in our own eyes, at the centre of the show.

It was not always thus. Religions traditionally declined to give human beings a pivotal or anointed place in the cosmos. The ancient Greeks pictured their Gods living on the summit of Mount Olympus and looking down upon humans with a mixture of amusement and pity. Zen Buddhism interpreted nature in general, with all its diverse flora and fauna, as far more important than any single creature, even one that mastered fire and language. And Judaism and Christianity presented the world 'theocentrically', with human life as a small, not-very-impressive fragment in a much larger scheme known only to the infinitely superior mind of God.

Our attention would, in the historic past, constantly have been drawn back to theocentric or biocentric perspectives. In ancient times, in the Parthenon, on the Acropolis above Athens, there stood a ten-metre-tall statue of Athena made of gold and ivory. No merchant, statesman or general, however accomplished in human terms, could look upon it and think of themselves as anything other than insignificant. In London, after the huge fire of 1666, the largest part of the city's revenue was assigned for decades to the building of St Paul's Cathedral: an edifice larger and more impressive than any other of the time. The Cathedral radiated across the city the fundamental idea that life on earth would be fleeting, our concerns slight and our personal triumphs petty in comparison to the glory of an omnipotent, omniscient and eternal God.

With the decline of religion we have come to embrace a philosophy of what we can term anthropocentrism: we have identified ourselves, as humans, as the most important things that exist. It's a move that can be cast as a liberation. The stories on which god-focused societies were founded have been displaced by tales of human heroism in business, science or the arts, but this liberation has brought an unexpected kind of suffering in its wake: a vicious sense of our own lack of importance as compared with that of certain esteemed others. It has unleashed a torrent of envy and inadequacy.

Theocentric or biocentric societies cast all our eyes upwards or sideways and attenuated destructive internecine feelings by reminding us that we were, every one of us, puny and forgettable propositions. However, there is now no established point of reference beyond us that can matter. What happens to us here and now is framed as overwhelmingly important; it is all there is. And so, everything that goes wrong, everything that frustrates or disappoints us, fills the horizon. The idea of something bigger, older, mightier, wiser and nobler than us to which we owe love and obedience has been stripped of its power to console us.

Religion, for its part, located the important events at distant points in time: in the age of myths and heroes or in the year 33 AD when Jesus was crucified. The events of our own days would be seen as mere ripples and minor accidents in the immense fabric of theological time. There was nothing very special about the present. Our natural instincts to panic and despair were reduced by being set within the grandest of perspectives.

The theocentric view of religion made it impressively clear that the so-called great figures in society were not really so great. They might have power over us, but they are nothing compared to divine authorities. The Greeks built stories into their culture, which they told themselves again and again in poems and plays, of how their greatest king, Agamemnon, was gruesomely punished by divine justice for the arrogance of his life. He was above all other people, but he was still a lowly subject of the Gods. The story was still being retold in the 18th century, when the German composer Gluck set the central words to music: 'great kings to whom all must bow, must themselves kneel before the Gods.'

A non-anthropocentric outlook allowed us to perceive ourselves as beautifully unimportant and rather ridiculous. How long we might live, whether we were very successful or not, how intelligent we were or how beautiful, would be absurd concerns from the point of view of a deity, Mount Olympus or the distant planets. We were invited, usefully, to see how unimpressive our merits all ultimately were.

In modernity, we have been left without these comforts and reliefs, tormented by a stupefyingly heavy sense of our own importance in a nevertheless wholly indifferent, random and unequal universe.

VII. ROMANTICISM

The modern era has been powerfully shaped by the notion that romantic love lies close to the meaning of life. The point of relationships is no longer just to help to rear children, pass assets down the generations or assure a tolerable friendship between two people: their point is to assure superlative contentment and spiritual and physical communion. Sexual relationships are not one kind of connection among others, they are – the ideology of Romanticism assures us – the only kind of connection worth valuing.

From the end of the 18th century onwards, there emerged, in the minds of poets and artists, a view of life which privileged sexual monogamous lifelong love over all other values. Angels, who had previously been believed to dwell in heaven, were relocated on earth and took up human form. We could all, with a little luck, find redemption through the love of a fellow member of our species.

With hugely good intentions, Romanticism encouraged us to place an impossible burden of expectation upon a partner. We would ask them to be our lover, our best friend, our confidant, our nurse, our financial advisor, our chauffeur, our co-educator, our social partner and our sex mate. And then, when they failed in a few of these roles, as they inevitably would, we were to interpret their inevitable imperfections as a sign, not that we had got to know someone properly, but that we had mistakenly come together with the wrong person.

Romanticism projected a set of beautiful ideas onto relationships. But the consequence of this ideology has been the discovery of extensive new ways of feeling dissatisfied, disappointed and ashamed around ourselves and our partners. It has made us a good deal more lonely – and notably less able to love.

VIII. NOVELTY

Modern societies assign immense prestige to whatever happens to be new. 'Progress' and 'innovation' are central terms of praise; to be 'old-fashioned' or 'out-of-date' is little short of a disaster.

One manifestation of this attitude is that we instinctively prefer youth to age. The ideal age is located roughly between nineteen and twenty-five, this is the cohort assumed to be at the heart of change: these are the people who have new ideas, new outlooks, new kinds of music and the right sort of spirit. Getting older is to move away automatically from novelty and hence goodness; we set ourselves up for decades of lamentation.

This contrasts radically with the outlook of traditional societies in which the young were admired only to the extent that they held out a promise of eventually becoming wise 'elders'.

Our modern devotion to novelty shows up additionally in our preoccupation with 'news'. News is our name for the information we think of as most important which is taken to be synonymous with what has happened in the last twenty-four hours – or the last five minutes. We conflate the recent with the significant. But, of course, this focus on the present cannot do justice to our needs, for the information we truly require might be located at more distant points in time. In order to live and die well, we might need to encounter 'news' from Socrates or Lorenzo de Medici, Schopenhauer or Jane Austen, but since these people have done nothing for decades or centuries, we're very unlikely ever to hear about them in our headlines.

Modernity's love of novelty is intended to grip our attention and bring excitement and connection into our lives; but by a strange twist of fate it often leaves us feeling superficial, fragmented, hollow and distracted.

–

This has not been a list of all that is wrong with the modern world; there are many additional political, economic, legal, administrative and cultural defects that could be mentioned. What's distinctive about the troubles we have discussed is that they are philosophical and psychological in nature: they concern our intimate sense of who we are and what our lives are about. They sit, therefore, in the area that religions have traditionally occupied. But they have not, it seems, been adequately addressed by the secular age. The task is to try to repurpose certain ideas from the religious past to help guide us – and to soothe our agitated and confused psyches.

※

III.

CONSOLATIONS

✳

To counter the ills of modernity, we propose – as part of an attempt to replace the insights of religion – eight leading ideas.

I. BROKENNESS

Although a generous and visionary idea, our belief in human perfectibility has driven us to collective disappointment and rage; we stand tormented by the notion that our problems could, with sufficient intelligence and effort, be rendered avoidable.

Our belief in perfectibility is very recent and strange in historical terms. For thousands of years, the inherent brokenness of the human animal was a cultural given. All substantial human endeavours – marriage, child-rearing, a career, politics – were understood to unfold against a backdrop of fundamental blunder and were accepted as sources of distinctive and elaborate misery. Buddhism described life itself as a vale of suffering; the Greeks insisted on the tragic structure of every human project;

Christianity characterised each of us as marked at birth by a divine curse.

Such gloomy outlooks feel, at first, as if they could only guarantee further misery. But in reality, they have the reverse effect. A philosophy of brokenness makes the many sorrows we will inevitably be subject to feel normal and hence more bearable; and casts any better eventuality as unlikely and, therefore, as something for which we can be intensely grateful.

In the late 4th century, as the immense Roman Empire was collapsing, the leading philosopher of the age, St Augustine, became deeply interested in possible explanations for the tragic disorder of the human world. One central idea he developed was what he legendarily termed *Peccatum Originale*: original sin. Augustine proposed that human nature is inherently damaged and tainted because – in the Garden of Eden – the mother of all people, Eve, sinned against God by eating an apple from the Tree of Knowledge. Her guilt was then passed down to her descendants and now all earthly human endeavours are bound to fail because they are the work of a corrupt and faulty human spirit. This odd idea might not be literally true, of course. However, as a metaphor for why the world is in a mess, it has a beguiling poetic truth, as relevant to atheists as believers. We should not – perhaps – expect too much from the human race, Augustine implies. We've been somewhat doomed from the outset. And that can, in certain moods, be a highly redemptive thought.

It is not hard to recast the concept of original sin in contemporary terms. It is not our souls that are broken but, as neuroscience teaches us, it is our minds. These minds, the faulty walnuts we interpret reality through, did not evolve in ways that render them easy companions in the harried conditions of modern life. Our emotions kick in before we've understood situations and swamp our fragile powers of reason; our appetites (for example, for sugar and sexual stimulation) are strong and insistent – and fatally attract us to things that no longer serve our best interests. Our childhoods bequeath to us all sorts of distortions which mar our ability to understand ourselves, communicate adequately and trust others. We emerge into adulthood with an extraordinary quota of debilitating quirks, blind spots, unhelpful obsessions, stark limitations, exaggerated worries, structural character flaws and distorted reasoning processes. And it's not just we who are broken: the same logic applies universally. We live in societies made up entirely of broken souls.

Our intelligence may give us a theoretical chance to straighten out our lives – modern technology is a testament to this – but stupidity is too deeply entrenched to be eradicated conclusively. Science will never be quite the answer we assume it will be. Our technology has a devilish habit of serving, rather than abetting, our folly. The dream of modernity was that stupidity would be eradicated by science and learning; instead, it seems that our intellectual capacities are fated to coexist alongside, and be inflamed by, our moral and psychological flaws. We remain barely evolved aggressive apes, in command of nuclear weapons.

With these dark facts in view, we should orient ourselves calmly towards ideas that will help us cope with our unavoidably broken natures. Self-acceptance bids us to accept without undue self-contempt or misery that we will – on a regular basis – commit gross errors, hurt those we care for, fail to seize opportunities and make irrational choices. We are not uniquely cursed, merely members of a predictably flawed race.

Aware of our proclivity to error, we should more graciously forgive those around us when they slip up. They (like us) were not evil so much as tired, overwrought, frightened and out of control; human, all too human. We should mobilise the idea of brokenness for the sake of generous, imaginative explanations of the less-than-ideal behaviour of others. An instinct for vengeance and moralism can give way to a keener readiness for patience and pity.

II. MELANCHOLIA UNIVERSALIS

A form of jolly optimism might sound like an ideal state of mind, but it has very little in common with what is truly required for a well-lived life. We would be advised to trust instead in a philosophy of universal melancholy, *melancholia universalis.*

A panoply of genuinely sad things will occur in every existence, pretty much every day. Fundamental sources of sorrow are everywhere: everything we love is vulnerable while most of what we are pained by is solidly established and resilient. We are condemned to have to leave the world with much of our business unfinished and many hopes unexploited. We won't have achieved even a small fraction of what at some points felt possible; we'll have missed an endless array of possibilities; we'll not have put our relationships into proper order, we will have countless reasons to be bathed in regret.

At the same time, there was no alternative. We are required to make decisions far in advance of experience or reliable data: we are steering blind. We had to decide on a career before we truly knew what a career might mean; we had to commit to another before we genuinely knew what a joint life would entail.

A war could have been avoided; an election could have gone a different way; an accident might not have happened; a cancer cell could have been benign; we might have fallen in with a different group of people when we were twenty-one; we might have had a more understanding boss; we could by chance have struck up a conversation with a wonderful stranger. We live in a universe of unknown options, of divergent futures and unexamined possibilities.

We each have a private version of these woes, but they are individual variations on what is ultimately a universal theme: the metaphysical sorrows of life. They arise because of life, not because of us. Whatever we do, whatever our situation, they will afflict us. No one escapes.

Non-optimistic cultures and religions have made the point central to their ideologies: 'life is suffering', in the Buddha's famous summation. To never have been born may be the greatest gift of all, said the Greek tragic playwright Sophocles. Christianity habitually described the world as a vale of tears. These profoundly sad summations were not intended to depress us. On the contrary a universal sense of melancholy was envisaged as a valid, redemptive element in a properly lived life.

The wisdom of the melancholy attitude (as opposed to the bitter or angry one) lies in the understanding that we have not been singled out, that our suffering belongs to humanity in general. Melancholy is marked by an impersonal take on suffering. It is filled with pity for the human condition.

We need a public culture that remembers how much of life deserves to have solemn and mournful moments and that isn't tempted – normally in the name of selling us things – aggressively to deny the legitimate place of grief. Melancholy is not rage or bitterness, it is a noble species of sadness that arises when we are open to the fact that life is inherently difficult for everyone and that suffering and disappointment are at the heart of human experience. It is not a disorder that needs to be cured; it is a tender-hearted, calm, dispassionate acknowledgement of how much pain we must inevitably travel through.

Melancholy isn't directly opposed to cheerfulness. If we accept that life is sad and difficult, we don't always have to stay tethered to this fact. We can open ourselves to the possibility of what might be called 'cheerful despair'. Despair can be the standard, tragic, expected background against which anything sweet, amusing and tender stands out and can be properly appreciated.

Once again, the ancient Greeks provided a useful model for thinking about this. They liked to contrast the attitudes of two philosophers: Democritus and Heraclitus. When they looked at the world Heraclitus was moved to tears, Democritus found himself laughing. Democritus laughed not out of naivety or indifference or cruelty but because he had already factored in a deeply sober and realistic account of all that is wrong with the world. He wasn't shocked that people are selfish, that we turn to violence when thwarted, that we make endless errors, that we are swayed by our appetites more than by our reason, that we betray one another, that we are sly and deceitful – all this was obvious to him. He laughed because he knew it all already – and had in the meantime spotted a few beautiful things to be content about and charmed by.

Ironically, gratitude becomes all the more powerful when we don't take the good in any way for granted. Armed with a philosophy of *melancholia universalis*, we can be genuinely delighted when someone is considerate or generous, patient or kind; we're thrilled when things happen, for once, to go well; the happiness of a dog chasing a stick can move us, because we know how rare unbounded joy is; many little sources of pleasure become dear to us because we grasp that they buck the trend of universal sorrow. We're less obsessed by what is missing from our lives and more grateful for that which is present and good. And so, 'little things' start to seem somewhat different; no longer a petty distraction from a mighty destiny, no longer an insult to ambition, but a genuine pleasure amidst a litany of troubles, an invitation to bracket anxieties and keep self-criticism at bay, a small resting place for hope in a sea of disappointment. We appreciate the friendly encounter, the long hot bath, the spring morning – and keep in mind how much worse it could always, and probably will one day, be.

III. DEPENDENCE

Individualism has made us sick; our consolation lies in a culture that properly respects the notion of dependence.

A philosophy of dependence acknowledges that we are not capable of achieving more than a fraction of what matters by ourselves. Our sense of who we are should therefore be focused not so much on our unique possessions and accomplishments but upon the many good things which have come to us largely through the efforts of others.

A striking incidental example of this attitude can be found in ancient Athens. In the 5th century BC, under the leadership of Pericles, the Athenians developed the idea that the public parts of their city should significantly surpass any private dwelling in terms of beauty and grandeur. They repudiated an attitude that would later be termed by the Roman historian Sallust *publice egestas, privatim opulentia* – public squalor and private opulence. They wanted public opulence and were willing to forgive private modesty. A home might be a simple wooden affair but the temple one visited twice a week would be majestically carved of limestone, the shopping area would be graceful and the theatres and gymnasiums would be places of charm and elegance. One's sense of pride wouldn't focus merely on what one had privately amassed but on how fine collective possessions happened to be. Self-esteem wouldn't depend on whether one had a nice dining room; it would matter so much more that a superb statue had been erected in the public square or that a new portico – where anyone could go to listen to Socrates and the sophists debating – had been built with unusually graceful ionic columns.

The contrast with our own times is painful. We find it almost impossible to imagine that a shopping centre might genuinely be more beautiful than a home or that new law courts could be visually more delightful than an upmarket beach resort – and hence that we could, with reason, be proud of the achievements of our society and not merely of our own private selves.

The Athenian view of public architecture is a specific point at which we meet the idea of dependence, with its belief that our sense of identity can legitimately be shored up by collective acts in which we may not have played any outstanding role.

But more intimately understood, the same idea of dependence arises as we recognise how much we owe our own development to the care and tenderness of others. Who we are is only very partially the result of our own toil. It has to do with the labour and continuous concern of parents, guardians and the collective more broadly. We can't be understood – and can't understand ourselves – as self-created monads or independent apparitions. We are always, to a vast extent, the undeserving recipients of the help of others and are the better for recognising this fact with modesty. It's a dependence that should be admitted with gratitude rather than buried in shame. The mummy's boy or girl may be criticised in a highly individualistic society, but they capture a sensitive and profound truth: that we all have an ongoing need for comfort and reassurance, whatever age we happen to be.

None of us can survive alone. In order to flourish, we can't look simply to our own unique strengths – we need to allow ourselves to be helped by, and therefore become dependent upon, the intelligence and talents of others. However accomplished we are, there will be areas of inevitable inadequacy: we may be sweet-natured, but not very strategic; we may be creative but a poor marketer of our own creations; we may be highly imaginative but lack the poise to make good decisions.

In a more collective, dependent vision of identity, a focus of pride emerges in the contribution we can make to the public, rather than individual, good. Our role may be quite small and yet entirely real. In the Middle Ages, when the cathedral of Chartres was being built, more or less the whole local population had a hand in the work. Someone might only be pushing a cart, carrying stone from the quarry or carving a tiny flower high up on a wall; they might be making lunch for the master masons or cutting timber for the scaffolding – but each was doing something that ultimately mattered for an immense final result. Their identity didn't focus simply on what 'I' did but on what 'we' could do together.

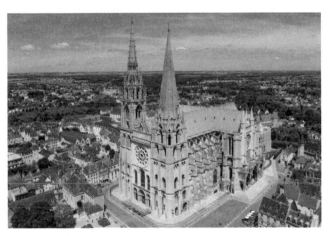

Chartres Cathedral: a sense of identity rooted in communal dependence.

It feels odd, for many people, to feel local or national pride. Being proud of one's city – which would have seemed obvious to a sophisticated ancient Greek – feels shameful and absurd to the educated modern imagination; loving one's country and being grateful to it gets recast as undignified, sinister nationalism.

But when we admit dependence into our picture of ourselves we take attention away from our own individual merits. We're not asking others to admire us solely for what we, personally, have done. We didn't make our city or our country, we didn't establish the company, we didn't bring ourselves up, we didn't teach ourselves to read and to think. A degree of modesty emerges. Our sense of who we are – our identity – becomes more expansive, more secure and less rooted in individual feats. And the buffetings of personal inadequacy count for proportionally less in the story of who we are. We can be full, valid people even if our own feats are limited and our powers circumscribed, because we're no longer forced to base our dignity on an impossibly narrow premise.

Unfortunately, it is nowadays not easy for us to find compelling counters to the logic of individualism. For multiple reasons the prestige of broad, dependent kinds of identity has been removed. We cannot feel good about ourselves by being members of a church (because it asks us to believe incredible things); we cannot pride ourselves on our families (because it seems parochial); we cannot define ourselves by our nation (because it feels chauvinistic); we cannot take pride in being, like the quarry workers at Chartres Cathedral, small cogs in a vast enterprise (because our corporations and institutions don't feel noble enough to warrant devotion).

We are thrown back on ourselves – but at the same time, conscious of our underlying frailty, we await the rediscovery of a plausible philosophy of dependence.

IV. ORDINARY LIFE

Modernity emphasises the glory of heroic achievement. It prizes excellence and disparages the norm. And it does so through the medium of art, understood in the widest sense; in adverts, films, magazines and novels, we are shown – often with great verve and skill – what is supremely impressive, appealing, intriguing and delightful about the lives of unusually successful people.

The contrast with our own lives could not be greater or more humiliating. But it is not the case that ordinary life is devoid of virtue, simply that we do not generally muster creativity and aesthetic energy to discover it. The consolation for our sense of comparative failure would be to look more accurately – with more sensitivity and more artistry – at the real beauty and sweetness of some of what surrounds us.

At various points in cultural history, important initiatives have been made in this direction. In the 1650s, the Dutch painter Johannes Vermeer painted a series of works in which he sought to show us what was appealing and honourable about ordinary activities: keeping a house tidy, sweeping the yard, babysitting, sewing or preparing lunch.

Johannes Vermeer, *The Milkmaid*, c.1657–1658

The woman featured in his *Milkmaid* has, perhaps, not had a moment to herself since she woke up; over the years she's only been able to accumulate a tiny nest egg; she's not her own boss; she's not especially proud of her looks. But to Vermeer she's a full and lovely individual. The painter was doing for her – and by extension for us – what, up to then, had mainly been done for generals, princes and popes: framing for both a moment and forever the genuine beauty and dignity of a unique being.

Johannes Vermeer, *The Little Street*, c.1657–1658

In another painting, Vermeer studied what might be appealing about living in a modest house in an unfashionable area of Delft. The paint is peeling from the window frames, no gilded carriage is ever going to roll up to the door; and they have to keep a close eye on the budget. But good lives unfold here nevertheless.

Vermeer was insisting that ordinary life is heroic in its own way, because ordinary-sounding things are very far from easy to manage. There is immense skill and true nobility involved in bringing up a child to be reasonably independent and balanced; maintaining a good-enough relationship with a partner over many years despite areas of extreme difficulty; keeping a home in reasonable order; getting an early night; doing a not-very-exciting or well-paid job responsibly and cheerfully; listening properly to another person; and, in general, not succumbing to madness or rage at the paradox and compromises involved in being alive.

Our misfortune is that the efforts of artists like Vermeer have been relatively unusual; the general tendency has been to make us experts in understanding the allure of the lives of the very few, while overlooking and underestimating the very real beauty, honour and appeal of the lives we are already living.

The process is endlessly repeated. For example, the best novelists make us see what could be lovely about lives entirely unlike our own: being a spy or a 19th-century aristocratic adventurer or a rebel general in a war in 2302. The real feat would be to take a life very much like ours, with its particular limitations, frustrations and enthusiasms, and render it desirable (which, in truth, it probably is).

The pleasures of our lives may look very minor – waking up early in summer, whispering in bed in the dark, talking to a grandparent, scanning through old photos – and yet be anything but. If properly grasped and elaborated upon, these sorts of activities may be among the most moving and satisfying we, or anyone, can have. It's just that a warm bath, an apple, a conversation with a close friend or a good night of sleep – lack prestige or social support. We don't feel we're living the *right* life, though we may in fact be living a *good* life.

The ordinary would, ideally, stop being a category of shame. We would fully and properly recognise how 'the ordinary' can also be fascinating, good, endearing, noble, dignified, fun, sexy, meaningful, desirable, complex, soothing, reassuring, surprising: indeed, all the things we only ever knew to look for in the extraordinary.

V. TRAGEDY

The ideology of meritocracy tells us that our outward status can be taken as an accurate reflection of our entire value as human beings. It is a philosophy that trusts in the possibility of moral justice in the here-and-now, in the status hierarchy: the good will be properly rewarded in this world, the bad will be reliably accorded what they have always deserved.

The concept of meritocracy renders failure not only materially hard, as it has always been, it makes it psychologically catastrophic in its levels of moral judgement. It denies us any possibility of metaphysical consolation; it leaves no room for any idea of 'bad luck'. There can be no one to blame but ourselves – and therefore, at points, no alternative but to loathe and perhaps do away with ourselves.

Yet we should note that not all societies and eras have seen success and failure in such stark and forbidding terms. In ancient Greece, another rather remarkable possibility – almost entirely ignored by our own era – was envisaged: you could be good and yet fail. To keep this idea at the front of the collective imagination, the ancient Greeks developed a particular art form: tragic drama. They put on huge festivals, which all the citizens were expected to attend, to act out stories of appalling, often grisly, failure. There was always a crucial premise built into these stories from the start: those upon whom failure so dramatically descended were shown to be really rather good people.

In a tragedy, decent, well-intentioned, capable souls were

shown making minor-seeming errors: they might break an obscure law without meaning to; they might misunderstand something someone said to them; they might draw the wrong conclusion from ambiguous evidence. They might simply have a moderate (and common) 'flaw' in their character: being a bit irascible, a touch arrogant or perhaps a little impatient.

And from this would flow disaster, calumny and the ultimate punishment. It would be the work of the playwright to show in detail how, from almost innocent, minor failings, catastrophe could advance by a series of plausible small steps. The ancient Greeks were offering themselves regular lessons that ran directly counter to an ideology of meritocracy. They were emphasising that if someone's life turns out badly, it is not a sure sign of an undeserving character. What happens is, to a large extent, in the hands of what the Greeks called 'fate' or 'the Gods' – their poetic manner of saying that things often work out in random ways, according to dynamics that don't simply reflect the merits of the individuals concerned.

Any society, such as ours, which is heavily invested in competition needs to supplement the idea of meritocracy with a realistic and sympathetic notion of tragedy. When we have failed, or when we see others have, we are often encountering the cruel workings of fate and chance. The person (who may also be us) who ends up defeated, alone, in trouble or impoverished may be – if only we could see the whole story properly – sensitive, serious, decent and very unlucky. And their unhappiness may properly deserve the compassion and kindness of all onlookers.

A strong, developed sense of tragedy is the necessary counterweight to competition. But our society currently lacks a powerful, wide-reaching and reliable institution for promoting a tragic – and hence compassionate – perspective on life. The Greeks had their public theatres, and, in the past, Christianity built its church around the story of a good man who, in worldly terms, got nowhere and met a degrading, agonising end.

By contrast, today we inhabit a culture that is more interested in humiliating those whose lives have already gone badly wrong than teaching us the art of tragedy. The natural appetite to condemn is stoked and feels correct – right up to the moment where misfortune strikes us and we are left alone with our sorrows in a hostile, mocking world.

VI. TRANSCENDENCE

Secular societies do not orient themselves around devotion to something bigger than, or beyond, themselves. They are not interested in what we can term transcendence: contact with eternal and grand phenomena in comparison with which our ordinary preoccupations can come to feel unimportant and redemptively insignificant in our own eyes.

With the receding of religion there is, in general, nothing left to awe or relativise us. Our immediate difficulties and burdens, our conflicts and pains are, it seems, all there is – and so they loom ever larger and more desperately in our agitated minds.

However, the sources of transcendence needn't be – as religions presumed – composed only of deities. They might involve the sight of the stars at night, spread out like diamonds on a mantle of velvety darkness: uncountable fiery suns, implausibly distant and themselves constituting only an infinitesimal fraction of the cosmos. We can begin to conceive how vanishingly minor our sun, our planet and we ourselves are in this sublime vastness. Imagined from sufficiently far away, all human differences fade. Our collective similarities seem more evident. Our conflicts and competitions feel less urgent or earnest.

Or it might be immersion in a desert that generates our sense of awe. Here, for hundreds of years very little has happened. History has been measured in inches of wind erosion; a boulder slipped from a hillside three hundred years ago. We're introduced to an epochal sense of time: it doesn't matter what we did yesterday or what we may do tomorrow. The normal scale of relevance we apply in our lives is suspended. The crags don't care who we are; they're not impressed, or disappointed, by our careers; they don't ask about our sex lives or our romantic histories. We are returned to a universal common denominator.

We might meet a hint of transcendence on a more domestic scale in a small animal, such as a duck or a hedgehog. Its life goes on utterly oblivious to ours. It is entirely devoted to its own purposes. The habits of its species have not changed for centuries. We may be looking intently at it, but it feels not the slightest curiosity about who we are; from its point of view, we are absorbed into the immense blankness of unknowable, incomprehensible things. A duck will take a piece of bread as gladly from a criminal as from a High Court judge; from a billionaire as from a bankrupt felon; our individuality is suspended – and it is an enormous relief.

Nature habitually envelops us in forces and sequences that are entirely above and beyond our control. The trees flower in spring and lose their leaves in autumn; the sea rises and falls; the earth spins around the sun bringing winter and summer, with no regard at all for us. And therefore our individual errors and our failings come to seem irrelevant: the processes of nature will continue with us or without us, whether we mess up or triumph, whether we have been mean or said something asinine. Nature does not upbraid us for being fools. A central task of culture should be to remind us that the laws of nature apply to us as well as to trees, clouds and cliff faces. Our goal is to become clearer about where our own tantalisingly powerful, yet always limited, agency stops – and where we will be left with no option but to bow to forces infinitely greater than ourselves.

Today, the transcendent is real, but disorganised and fragmented. Religions organised it, interpreted it, ensured our regular contact with it, took it to the centre of shared public culture and insisted on its importance.

There continue to be opportunities to meet the transcendent but for the moment they seem to be left to individual chance. The power to bring a consoling perceptive to our troubles is not harnessed by any powerful institution that has our best interests in view. The consolation is there, but we live unconsoled, waiting for the transcendent to be mastered and applied to our inner squalls and sorrows.

VII. GOOD ENOUGH

High ambitions are noble and important, but there can also come a point when they become the sources of terrible trouble and unnecessary panic, creating a standard of judgment against which our actual lives are bound to fail. Our Romanticism – which sounds so impressive when expressed in art or song – can ruin our chances of maintaining decent, realistic relationships in the world we actually live in.

An important corrective to this attitude was developed by the mid-20th-century British psychiatrist and psychoanalyst Donald Winnicott. In his clinical practice, Winnicott often encountered parents who were deeply worried that they weren't doing a good job of bringing up their children. What struck Winnicott was that, almost always, these were actually good and loving people. They weren't perfect, of course. They might be rather busy, a bit short-tempered at times or anxiously juggling divergent commitments. But, in all sorts of basic ways, they were what he came to term 'good enough.'

The notion of 'good enough' can be usefully extended across many facets of life and, in particular, relationships. A marriage may be 'good enough' even in its darkest moments. Perhaps at times there's little sex and a lot of arguments; there are areas of loneliness and non-communication. Yet at the same time there are zones of tenderness, kindness and understanding. Instead of being tormented by the imperfections of love, under the aegis of a 'good enough' philosophy, we can worry less. Actual relationships are never ideal, but they can often offer us enough to get on with our lives.

Couples who compromise are not the enemies of love: they may be at the vanguard of understanding what lasting relationships truly demand. They deserve admiration, not condemnation. At its heart, compromise is a recognition that the ideal is not actually on offer; we're not stupidly or timidly backing down when we might have attained perfection with an extra push. By compromising, we're honouring how much of the good is actually attainable, given the constraints of a reality we are newly devoted to respecting.

VIII. RECURRENCE

Modernity is preoccupied by novelty, to our cost, for much that we are and love is not new. The compensation – and consolation – we need lies in carefully reminding ourselves of the balancing importance of things that are recurring and cyclical.

When we focus on recurrent history, rather than the news of today, we stand to discover that crises and emergencies, disasters, corruption and incompetence are standard features – to some degree – of all societies. Of course we want things to go better, but if we focus on recurrence we have a wiser sense of what improvements plausibly look like. We won't be drawn to dramatic solutions, we'll be more patient with small-scale, boring-sounding incremental steps; we'll not be too dismayed by inevitable setbacks.

If we look at enough relationships through the lens of recurrence, we will similarly start to realise that there are issues that standardly arise, and therefore are likely to feature in our own loves as well.

If we look at enough careers in detail, here too we will discover just how much difficulty and pain lie behind all achievements.

That problems occur is not the fault of anyone in particular. They are tied to quite basic features of the human condition: our limited self-knowledge; the fact that we must take decisions from a position of ignorance via our faulty minds. We may temporarily stave off or sidestep problems, but they will always make a return to our lives in some form. They belong to the cyclical downturns of the human condition.

Nature is perhaps the supreme teacher of the idea of recurrence. By studying it, we are continually meeting the same patterns: a tree puts out its first buds; it blossoms and comes into leaf; its fruit ripens and falls; the leaves change colour, wither and are blown away by the wind, leaving the branches bare. Our lives are at points no less circumscribed and subject to necessity. Concentrating on the recurrent patterns of nature primes us to understand the structure of our own embodied lives.

We should not expect to have mysteriously escaped the laws of existence. We remain part of the cycle of time. There is, thankfully, little that is ever entirely new.

*

CREDO

*

Religions have always understood that one of the greatest problems of our minds is that we know so much in theory about how we should behave and feel but engage so little with our knowledge in our day-to-day conduct.

We know – in theory – about resisting perfectionism, accepting melancholy, embracing an ordinary life, keeping room for the idea of tragedy and looking beyond anthropocentrism. And yet, in practice, any such ideas have a notoriously weak ability to motivate our actual behaviour and emotions. Our knowledge is both embedded *within* us and yet is ineffective *for* us.

We forget almost everything. Our memories are sieves, not robust buckets. What seemed a convincing call to action at 8 a.m. will be nothing more than a dim recollection by midday and an indecipherable contrail in our cloudy minds by evening. Our enthusiasms and resolutions can be counted upon to fade like the stars at dawn. Nothing much sticks.

The ancient Greeks were unusually alert to this phenomenon and gave it a helpfully resonant name: *akrasia*, commonly translated as 'weakness of will'. It was, they proposed, because of akrasia that we have such a tragic proclivity for knowing what to do but not acting upon our own best principles.

There is a solution to these fragilities of mind that religions knew to draw upon: ritual. Ritual can be defined as the structured repetition of important concepts, made resonant through the help of formal pageantry and ceremony. Ritual takes thoughts that are known but unattended and renders them active and vivid once more in our distracted minds. Unlike standard modern education, ritual doesn't aim to teach us anything new – it wants to lend compelling form to what we believe we already know. It wants to turn our theoretical allegiances into habits.

It is, not coincidentally, religions that have been especially active in the design and propagation of rituals. It is they that have created occasions at which to tug our minds back to honouring the seasons, remembering the dead, looking inside ourselves, focusing on the passage of time, empathising with strangers, forgiving transgressions or apologising for misdeeds. They have put dates in our diaries to take our minds back to our most sincere commitments.

We might interpret rituals negatively, as symbols of an old-fashioned attempt to control and direct our thoughts by appointment. But the best rituals don't so much impose ideas upon us that we are opposed to; they take us back to ideas we are in deep agreement with but have allowed to lapse: they are an externally mandated route to inner authenticity.

In the course of secularising our societies, we may have been too hasty in doing away with rituals. An education system alive to the wisdom of religions would perceive the role of structured lessons that constantly repeat what we know already – and yet so arduously and grievously forget. A good 'school' shouldn't tell us only things we've never heard before; it should be deeply interested in rehearsing all that is theoretically known yet practically forgotten.

–

Part of getting ideas to stick is to try to reduce them down to an essence. To stand any hope of remaining with us, theses need to be brief. The above delineation of eight consoling ideas may fit academic protocols and meanders at a pace that would suit someone on a substantial train journey, but stands no chance in the more hurried conditions of ordinary life. We need to boil things down much further – we need things to fit on the backs of postcards.

A table makes a good start:

Modern Ideals	Consoling Virtues
1. PERFECTIBILITY	BROKENNESS
2. OPTIMISM	MELANCHOLIA UNIVERSALIS
3. INDIVIDUALISM	DEPENDENCE
4. EXCEPTIONALISM	ORDINARY LIFE
5. MERITOCRACY	TRAGEDY
6. ANTHROPOCENTRISM	TRANSCENDENCE
7. ROMANTICISM	GOOD ENOUGH
8. NOVELTY	RECURRENCE

This can be accompanied by eight capsule summaries, which can be turned to and repeated at moments of difficulty. We shouldn't merely focus emotional education on elaborate things we've never heard of before; we should systematically rehearse basics that are theoretically known to us yet practically always in danger of being forgotten.

1 BROKENNESS

We are inherently flawed and broken beings.

Perfection is beyond us.

Despite our intelligence and our science, we will never stamp out stupidity and pain. Life will always continue to be – in central ways – about suffering.

We are all, from close up, scared, unsure, full of regret, longing and error.

We are not unusual in our follies. The only people we can think of as 'normal' are those we don't yet know very well.

Recognition of our inherent madness, weakness and error should not be a source of shame. From it flows compassion for ourselves and generosity towards others.

Knowing how to reveal our vulnerability and brokenness is the beginning of compassion and friendship.

2 MELANCHOLIA UNIVERSALIS

We are under undue and unfair pressure to smile.

But grief is our more natural, and more consoling home.

Nothing good will be easy or go entirely well: We can expect frustration, misunderstanding, misfortune and rebuffs.

Though there is a vast amount to feel sad about.
We're not individually cursed.

Against the backdrop of sorrow
The small sweet things stand out:
A sunny day, a drifting cloud;
Dawn and dusk,
A tender look ...

We can believe in cheerful despair.

3   DEPENDENCE

We did not make ourselves unaided.
We are dependent creatures.
We're loyal to a bigger understanding of our lives.

From the start, as children
We needed the kindness and help of others
And we still do.
We need the mercy of a second chance,
We need encouragement,
We need forgiveness because none of us
Can stand the severest truths of who we are and
what we've done.

We can take pride in belonging to things bigger
that ourselves.
We can love what we belong to
Though it doesn't just belong to us.
We can be proud of what others have done for us
And not only of what we've done for ourselves.

4   ORDINARY LIFE

We are not heroes; we recognise ourselves as
ordinary
And are committed to seeing the merits of our
ordinary lives.

We see what is lovely, sweet, good and important
About simple and commonplace things.
'Ordinary' isn't a name for failure.
Understood more carefully,
And seen with a more generous and
perceptive eye,
It contains the best of life.

Life is not elsewhere; is it, fully and properly,
Here and now.

5   TRAGEDY

People do not reliably end up with the lives they
deserve.
There is no real justice in the way that rewards are
distributed.
We are subject to appalling whims of chance and
ill luck.

We should embrace the idea of tragedy.
We see that terrible things can and do befall lives.
A small mistake, a minor flaw can lead to horror:
Someone like us could be bankrupt, in jail or
vilified in the press.

We can fail and be good;
All the tragedies of others live in embryo in us.

We need to be slower to judge and quicker to
understand.
Those who have failed are not 'losers'.
We may soon be among them.

6   TRANSCENDENCE

We are not at the centre of anything; thankfully.
We are minuscule bundles of matter on an
infinitesimal corner of a boundless universe.
We do not count, in the grander scheme.

We need the relief of a cosmos that doesn't care –
The kindly indifference of infinity:
An eternity where no one will notice
Where the wind erodes the rocks,
In the space between the stars.

Silence and humility are a blessing
After a life of jostling and anxious pride.

7   GOOD ENOUGH

Anyone we could love would frustrate us
profoundly over time.
True love isn't about admiring perfection; it is
about being charitable to what is weak and broken.

A feeling of compatibility should not be a
precondition of love;
It is its consequence.

We will at points wish our partners dead and think
the day we met them the worst of our lives.
And at other points, we will recognise them as
being very much good enough.

'The one' is a cruel invention.
No one is ever 'right'. But being a little wrong isn't
the end of anything;
It's the only true basis upon which lasting love can
be built.

8   RECURRENCE

We get transfixed by the new
But most of life has happened before:
The giant wheel keeps turning.

Love is difficult,
Work is hard,
Societies are mad,
Politics goes wrong,
No one is loved as much as they deserve,
Everyone is lonely and afraid;
There's nothing weirder than being alive –
Then we sicken and we die.

The more we concentrate
On novelty
The harder it is to hear the vital things
Which may have happened long ago.

We need a culture that can remind us
Often enough
And in ways we can bear to hear
Of the older things we very much still need to
know.

V.

ARCHITECTURE

✳

It is one of the odder features of our psychology that we are different people in different places. The built environment hugely influences how we feel about ourselves, our communities and the purpose of our lives. In certain buildings, our mood is serene and uplifted, in others, it tugs towards the depressed or the sterile. Architecture plays a critical role in enabling us to be a certain way.

It is perhaps for this reason that religions have long involved themselves in architecture. In their quest to mould our inner lives, they have deemed it relevant to place us, often at huge cost, in specific architectural contexts: to take a deep interest in what the ceiling should be like, what the views should give out on to and what the walls should be made of. Architecture has been honoured as one of several leading non-intellectual ways in which we can be educated into being particular sorts of people.

We do not need to believe in the faiths to have a broad sense of what particular religious works are attempting to do to our souls. The English 19th-century critic John Ruskin remarked that all works of architecture 'speak' to us and we can sense their discourse easily enough; when we walk into the Sheikh Loftollah Mosque in Iran, we intuit that our minds are being directed upwards towards something that appears sublime and ineffable, just as we can feel, on a wooden platform of the Rozan-ji Temple in Japan, an invitation to a modest kind of calm and reconciliation with the natural world.

The most secular audiences are often left in awe by the great examples of religious architecture. We may be utterly indifferent towards the faith-based aspects of religions, and yet still moved by the profundity, intricacy and elegance of many mosques, temples, cathedrals and churches.

However, any nostalgia for religious buildings tends to be cut short by the sense that an end to belief must inevitably mean an end to the possibility of putting up anything that might reflect the ambitions of religious buildings. We cannot – so the thinking goes – be interested in putting up 'temples' if we don't have any gods to worship.

Yet on closer examination, it in no way logically follows that an end to our devotion to sacred beings must mean an end to temples. We can plausibly retain an interest in buildings whose primary purpose is to 'speak' to us about certain psychological or ethical ideas (rather than to house or

Sheikh Lotfollah Mosque, Isfahan, Iran:
an essay on the sublimity and power of God.

Rozan-ji Temple, Kyoto, Japan:
an invitation to calm and reconciliation with nature.

shelter us). In the absence of gods, we still retain a longing for serenity, for community, for grandeur, for sweetness, for perspective – all of which are values and themes that can be celebrated and enhanced through architecture. There is no reason why we should not continue to build secular structures that, like the temples and cathedrals of old, skilfully generate feelings of awe, gratitude, wonder, mystery and silence; buildings that bring us together for special moments of the year, where we can mark key stages of our lives, and where we can be taken out of the everyday and encouraged to regain a sense of perspective or nurture a feeling of communal affection.

It must, in other words, remain logically possible to have 'temples' without gods; temples not to this or that deity but to particular *ideas*. By a temple, we simply mean a work of architecture that, over and above any practical material purpose, sets out to foreground a mood or outlook.

In a world that learnt to secularise more wisely, we would not be seeking to do away with temples; rather, we would want to continue to build temples to values that feel both important and yet constantly under threat.

We have, over previous chapters, identified eight consoling ideas with which to combat some of the leading ills of modernity. From this set of eight, we can imagine commissioning a range of temples:

- a temple for brokenness
- a temple for melancholy
- a temple for dependence
- a temple for ordinariness
- a temple for tragedy
- a temple for transcendence
- a temple for the good enough
- a temple for recurrence

There is no need to define exactly what each temple should look like here. In the case of religions, those who commissioned buildings were not themselves architects and never claimed to be able to determine the details of the structures they wanted to exist for the well-being of their followers. They were theologians or philosophers first and foremost and their talents lay in defining *what* they wished their buildings to do to our souls – not in their insight into exactly *how* they might affect these desired changes. They wrote a spiritual–ethical brief, but then deferred to the architects in their locality to translate it into a relevant architectural idiom.

For example, most Christian architectural briefs have proposed the creation of buildings that would make Jesus' message of love, kindness and community resonant in our hearts, but architects have on this basis erected structures as different as St Michael's Church in Bavaria on the one hand, or the Urnes Stave Church in Norway on the other.

St Michael's Church, Bavaria

Urnes Stave Church, Norway

In a similar vein, it is not our task to say quite what a new kind of secular temple should look like – it is simply to specify what its psychological impact on a user should be.

A set of briefs might run as follows:

A TEMPLE FOR BROKENNESS

A building to reconcile us with our broken, imperfect selves and to celebrate the impossibility of perfection in human life.

A TEMPLE FOR MELANCHOLY

A building to provide a refuge against the over-optimism of contemporary society and to create a home for moods of tender sadness and grief.

A TEMPLE FOR DEPENDENCE

A building to acknowledge our longing for community, to celebrate group effort and counterbalance an otherwise often exhausting need for individual glory and supremacy.

A TEMPLE FOR ORDINARINESS

A building that points us towards the overlooked value and importance of modesty and domesticity.

A TEMPLE FOR TRAGEDY

A building to which we might repair in moments of failure

and disgrace, in order to recover a feeling that we continue to be worthy of charity and love; a building to temper the force of our self-hatred and the condemnation of a judgemental world.

A TEMPLE FOR TRANSCENDENCE

A building to remind us of the negligible place we occupy in time and space; a building that can attenuate our worries and egoistic concerns by placing us in a newly vast context which fruitfully diminishes us in our own eyes.

A TEMPLE FOR THE GOOD ENOUGH

A building which is properly 'Romantic' in the sense of fostering in us the skills needed to appreciate and keep faith with our partners; a building which acknowledges the difficulty of relationships while helping to equip us with the skills and attitudes needed to manage them.

A TEMPLE FOR RECURRENCE

A building which works against the contemporary obsession with novelty and reminds us of the cyclical nature of existence, calming our frenzied minds and putting us in touch with the deeper, recurring patterns of nature and history.

These briefs, handed to a range of architects (across geographies, age groups, budgets and climates) would be expected to result in a great variety of buildings. The temples might be perched on hillsides and hewn of marble or limestone; or they could be gigantic halls standing out on the horizon of cities or modest wooden huts in a forest clearing. They might make use of the most advanced technologies or purposefully rely on immemorial materials and construction methods. But beneath these different outward interpretations, an underlying intellectual coherence would be maintained: these would all be buildings that attempted to correct, through the medium of architecture, certain psychological ills of modernity.

—

To expand on this idea, let's consider in greater detail what could be done with the sixth of the eight briefs above: a temple for transcendence.

The overall purpose of this building would be to assuage our customary tendencies to exaggerate our own importance, with all the painful consequences that result. The building would need to evoke for us just how small we are when considered against the vastness of the cosmos or the aeons of time since the origins of the universe.

Having given the brief to an architectural practice, we can imagine a temple for transcendence in the form of a huge thin tower, clad in roughly hewn black granite that could hold only a few people in it at any one time. Its height would represent the age of the earth, with each centimetre of height equating to one million years. Measuring forty-six metres in all, the tower would have, at its very base, a tiny band of gold only one millimetre thick, which would stand for mankind's time on earth – and the eye would be invited upwards to consider what a brief and puny phenomenon homo sapiens truly is. One would, in such a space, be returned to a pleasing impression of one's nullity in the greater scheme – while the sight of the tower across the city skyline would be a permanent reminder to the busy, egoistic citizens to remember the ultimately insignificant nature of their worries, jealousies and fears.

This would be only one of many possible ways of interpreting the brief for the temple for transcendence. What matters above all in the exercise is the recovery of an idea that was unfairly lost, to our great collective cost, in the process of secularisation: the notion that a lack of gods to worship would have to mean the end of attempts to create 'temples', spaces with the express purpose of affecting our mood, priorities and sense of self.

It remains eminently open to us to use architecture to remind us of our psychological allegiances and to battle against what threatens to weary and demean us. The

Tom Greenall and Jordan Hodgson,
A Temple to Perspective

love and talent that flowed into religious architecture
need not dry up with the death of our gods, because we
have not ceased to harbour values we cherish and need
reminding of.

We can look forward to a new secular era, every bit as
creative as the ecclesiastical one that preceded it, in which
we restore architecture to its rightful place as a supreme
medium through which to celebrate our ethical and

psychological commitments and ask our buildings to help us to become (or remain) who we truly want to be.

*

VI.

ART

*

Across centuries, in all parts of the world, religions have taken the arts very seriously: the Greeks, Romans and Hindus made statues of their gods; Islamic calligraphy presented sacred texts in an artistic form; Buddhism sponsored countless statues of the serene face of its inspirational founder; and Christianity produced large numbers of paintings of key moments in the life of Jesus. Most of what we consider to be great art is, in one way or another, the result of religious patronage.

It is no accident that religions have been so heavily concerned with art. At their core, religions have sought to get us to care about ideas. They want us to remember the Buddha's teachings and understand the power of Shiva; to keep in mind the importance of humility for Mohammed and to stay faithful to Christ's commandments about love.

But they have also been confronted by a basic problem with how our minds work. We tend not to take ideas in properly unless they have first been presented to us in an emotionally appealing and seductive way. It is not enough for an idea to be true; if it is to stick in our minds, it will have to be rendered sensuously tempting as well. Because the ideas that we most need to hear are usually the ones that we would in some ways like to ignore, we need the toughest lessons to be coated in the most subtle and inventive charm. As religions grasped, we need an alliance of education and seduction. At certain historical moments, this point has been well heeded. The central philosopher of the Renaissance, Marsilio Ficino, wished to teach the population of Florence to live according to the highest principles of virtue and intelligence. But he also knew the human mind well; he understood that it was no use delivering lectures if genuine change on a large scale was required. And so he persuaded his patrons, the wealthy Medici family, to harness the seductive skills of Italy's finest artists to a broad and subtly concealed educational programme: he asked artists to become teachers. Magnificent buildings and appealing works of art were allied to the noblest lessons of classical and Biblical authors. Annunciations, nativities and descents from the cross became both artistically mesmerising and philosophically compelling.

Religions understand that we are sensuous and emotional creatures long before we are intellectual ones. A pure thought on its own cannot easily make its way to the centre of our minds. We will too easily lose touch with a complex idea if we merely hear about it in a lecture or a sermon. In order for ideas to take up an important place in our lives, they need first to astonish our senses.

Sandro Botticelli, *Lamentation over the Dead Christ*, c.1490: a lesson in tragedy wrapped in artistic genius.

The urge to nag is very understandable, especially when a lesson is important. But sadly, nagging – the insistent, urgent, graceless repetition of a message – will only ever work for a small number of people who are almost on side anyway. It cannot change humanity. What naggers have to say may be supremely important, but their manner of delivery ensures it will never be heard.

Seduction through art is the alternative to nagging.

Religions have long proposed that the seductive techniques of art should be carefully deployed to make sure that what really matters reliably works its way into the hearts and minds of pretty much everyone.

Distinctively, religions did not think it was the task of artists to work out *what* their art should talk to us about. They did not want artists to be thinkers; merely the popularisers and promoters of the ideas of others. Religions already had a philosophy or a creed – they weren't asking artists to come up with their own original themes. They operated with a clear division of labour: religions were to come up with the ideas, artists were to give them a sensuous form.

This division wasn't insulting or limiting to artists themselves. Arguably, it set them free to do what they were best at. The individual personality, style, talent and imagination of the artist was still hugely important; there was room for originality of execution, but none at the level of intellectual direction.

In Buddhism, for instance, artists were asked again and again to make more or less the same images of the Buddha, but this still allowed individual artists to bring richness and nuance to the interpretations of their task.

A Buddha produced in Thailand around the 15th century,

could be subtly very different from an equally beautiful one made in Sri Lanka three hundred years later – even if both obeyed the overall mission of bringing to life the peacefulness and charity at the heart of the Buddha's teachings.

Seated Buddha,
Thailand, 15th century

Buddha,
Sri Lanka, 18th century

Likewise, Christian artists were given a heavily prescribed list of central moments in Jesus' life, but within these parameters were allowed a large amount of leeway in the way they might interpret these. A rendition of Jesus washing his disciples' feet – a lesson to promote the idea of humility – might be as varied as one painted by Tintoretto in the 16th century or Ford Madox Brown in the nineteenth.

Tintoretto, *Christ Washing the Disciples' Feet*, 1549

Ford Madox Brown, *Jesus Washing Peter's Feet*, 1856

Because the old religions have faded from our lives, we have come to assume that their approach to art couldn't now be relevant. And yet the opposite is true. We can distinguish between the precise agendas of religions on the one hand – and their ambitious and helpful vision of the role of art on the other. The broad didactic approach employed by religions needn't fall victim to the secular temper of our times. Rather than leaving the question of what art should be about only to the inspiration of individual artists, there remains a role for formulating a systematic agenda of topics that contemporary artists should address, an agenda established by non-artists and focusing on mankind's ongoing search for consolation, self-understanding and fulfilment.

Based around an analysis of the ills of modernity and of the balancing, consoling ideas that help us cope with them, we can draw up a project for the arts that can stand comparison with the mighty commissioning projects of religions. We can identify, across a range of psychological areas, the kinds of themes to which artists should give sensuous expression. Such an agenda would return art to its proper place at the centre of our lives – because it would be a primary way in which we would meet the ideas that can most help us.

Sculpture and painting happened to be traditional areas

that religious art focused on in the past, but the use of these media were historic accidents. Today, the sensuous embodiment of ideas could just as well make use of other complimentary artistic forms: films, documentaries, paintings, photos, comic books, installations, performance art and so on. It is not ultimately the medium that matters but the effect on the audience, the way that a good, helpful idea we need can be gently and alluringly drawn to the centre of our minds and of our lives.

We can imagine a commissioning agenda set for artists by psychologist–philosophers, focused on the eight sources of consolation previously identified.

I.

ART FOR BROKENNESS

• Under this heading would sit works of art that could help to reconcile us with our broken and imperfect nature, that would liberate us from the folly of perfectionism and render it safer to share our vulnerabilities with others.

• A work might show us an encounter with a person with an outwardly successful life who nevertheless harboured profound inner shame and despair. We would be coaxed into feeling less alone with the darker parts of ourselves and readier to imagine the turmoil beneath the confident or impassive surfaces of other people.

• Works could lend their prestige to our admission of our own strangeness and idiocy and model for us how to reveal our brokenness (our odder, more disturbed aspects) in ways that did not frighten or hurt others.

• A work could gently undermine the boosterish assumptions of our technological age and teach us to accept fragilities, reversals, ongoing chaos and follies as ineradicable features of the human project. We could accept that our species can perfectly imagine, but never, for that matter, build itself, a paradise – and that life becomes a great deal more tolerable once we reconcile ourselves to, and work around, this dark, stubborn fact.

II.

ART FOR MELANCHOLIA UNIVERSALIS

• Under this heading would come works that sombrely acknowledged how much we have to be sad about and could thereby attenuate our anger and disappointment at the frequently disappointing nature of reality.

• Works would take care to communicate that grief and frustration are not personal curses but are written into the contract of existence: we have not been damned, we are simply experiencing part of the accidents and sorrows that come with being alive.

• Works would convert tears of rage into melancholy. The mood would be elegiac. We would see that suffering belongs to us all and is what binds us together rather than what isolates us.

• Works would counter the suffocating optimism prevalent in commercial society; they would give a dignified home to our more downbeat states. They would make it easier for each one of us to come to terms with our darkness and to reach out to similarly afflicted strangers.

III.

ART FOR DEPENDENCE

• The temper of modernity pushes us to assert our individuality and celebrate our unique prowess. Works in this category would highlight how much we owe to others and continue to need the support and reassurance we relied on when we were younger. They would rehabilitate the idea of dependence.

• A work might bring out how much our childhood needs for comfort and reassurance have survived into adulthood and should not be sources of shame or denial.

• A work might explore the deep-seated anxieties generated in us by a philosophy of individualism – and provide catharsis and reassurance around it.

• A work would show us how much richer our identities are than merely what we happen to do to earn money – and how shaky the connection is between outward success and virtue.

• A work could give sympathetic expression to our desire for collective pride – that is, our longing to belong to something larger than ourselves and to contribute meaningfully to our communities, nations and planet.

IV.

ART FOR ORDINARY LIFE

• Works of art under this heading would assuage our feelings that life is somehow always elsewhere, and that glamour and importance reside where we are not.

• They would enhance the prestige of ordinary life, by which is meant life as most citizens in a given country are forced to lead it, and which tends to differ so markedly from the mediatised representations we otherwise receive.

• Works might reveal the quiet heroism involved in simply keeping going, in managing a job tolerably well, in bringing up a family, in not giving way to rage and anxiety, in forgiving and accepting what cannot be changed.

• Works would reawaken us to the existence of many small pleasures which can bring us solace in darker moments.

V.

ART FOR TRAGEDY

• This art form would remind us of how easy it is for

more or less good people to make small errors that end up unleashing catastrophe.

• The art would teach us to feel sympathy for others and fear for ourselves, in a way that would expand our humanity and make us less rigidly judgemental. We would move beyond words like fool, pervert, weirdo and loser towards an appreciation of the richness, complexity and troubled goodness inside almost everyone.

• Tragic art would counterbalance the otherwise prevalent moralistic mood and remind us of how much compassion is required in order for a society to function humanely.

VI.
ART FOR TRANSCENDENCE

• This would be an art that would draw us away from our more petty and egoistic concerns and remind us – in a kind and redemptive way – of our insignificance and puniness in the wider scheme.

• We would be reminded of the negligible position we occupy in the cosmos and the brevity of the here-and-now within the aeons of time since creation.

• Works of art would generate feelings of pleasing awe, in which we would be impressed and fruitfully humbled by the beauty and majesty of natural phenomena.

• We might encounter typically ignored animals, remote

vistas, foreign planets – or long-distant periods of history.

• The purpose would always be to transcend the bounds of our own egos in order to help us appreciate the pleasing indifference of the totality in which we reside.

VII.

ART FOR GOOD ENOUGH RELATIONSHIPS

• A great deal of the art presently created subscribes to a Romantic philosophy of relationships, which implicitly suggests that it is within our remit to find a kind of love that fuses together practical support, emotional connection, sexual excitement, parental obligations and lifelong fulfilment.

• Art under this category would work in an opposite direction. It would propose that Romanticism has been the enemy of our capacity to succeed at relationships and that love is, first and foremost, a skill to be learnt, not an emotion to be felt.

• This art would help us to deal with the ordinary travails and challenges of love, not to panic at what is hard, to distinguish between fantasy and reality, to unpick the legacies of childhood and to render us more resilient and good-humoured in the face of the often appalling difficulties involved in living alongside even a very fine example of a human for any length of time.

• This would be an art that would reconcile us with the

idea of relationships that could be, not perfect, but very much worth treasuring nevertheless, relationships that would be triumphantly yet modestly 'good enough.'

VIII.
ART FOR RECURRENCE

• This would be art that would pull us away from our concerns with what is novel and over-stressed by the medium we tellingly call 'the news'.

• It would seek to balance us inwardly through exposure to what is ancient, recurring and cyclical – with a view to offering us inner calm, perspective and maturity.

• Works might lean on a study of natural phenomena which would impressively induct us into the lifecycle to which all living things are subject.

• Another kind might remind us of the multiple stages through which all civilisations progress, and the waxing and waning of all things in the cosmos.

–

Under such headings, artworks could be generated which would carry an explicit intention to deal more wisely with the ills to which our times subject us. They would allow us to repeatedly meet the ideas we need, framed within emotionally stirring and memorable forms, so that they would better lodge themselves in our individual minds and in our collective culture.

*

VII.

THE PRIESTLY FUNCTION

✳

A notable feature of religions is that they haven't traditionally simply dispensed their advice through books or sermons. They have had people on the ground, with whom their audiences could have conversations about what troubled them most at key moments of their lives; they had priests.

These priests might be distinguished by special clothing; they would receive extensive training and usually they were professional – in the sense that their religions provided them with their chief source of income.

There were a range of priestly functions that these groups evolved to carry out. For instance, they would traditionally choreograph collective moments of transcendence for their communities. They would lead a sacred dance or perform a ceremony invoking eternal and universal themes. Or they might be specialists in interpretation. At the temple of Delphi in ancient Greece, the priests tried to make sense of puzzling, disturbing or strange experiences – although the interpretations they offered can sound strange to us today (they might tell you that a dream meant you had to find a new city).

Another priestly function was to help us individually confront our brokenness. This role was developed particularly in the Catholic ritual of confession. In deep privacy, the priest would listen to – and carefully enquire about – someone's account of the things they'd done wrong in their lives. Making a confession to a priest was a way of lessening the burden of guilt, via a sincere feeling of sorrow, to regain the strength to be a more moral and kind human being going forward. In secret, an individual could admit to themselves – and to one other person – that they really had been unfair or unkind or very harsh. They could admit their errors and their feelings of remorse could be properly witnessed.

Priests would help their audiences to mingle and open their hearts to one another. They would arrange occasions when it was possible to make new friends and show vulnerability and kindness to other members of the community. They would function as 'hosts', setting rules in their jurisdictions whereby interactions between people would be more sincere and less status-focused.

The priestly mission was seldom centred on the rich and the successful. The idea was that everyone's soul was of equal value to God. The priest would listen as attentively to the sins or woes of the stable boy as to those of the local landowner. They were agents of a point of view in which social status didn't reflect the real worth of a person. In the eyes of the priest the great acts of life could be going on in a humble cottage. The priest was the personal representative of the idea that we do not need to be special, famous, successful or outstanding at something to be loved by God.

Individual priests might not have performed these functions very well – and they were operating with a set of ideas about the will of God or the importance of heaven that many of us would now find it hard to believe in. But for a long time, and for many people, they did provide some consolation for, and help with, the trials of existence. At critical junctures in a life, one called for the priest long before one asked for the doctor.

With the decline of religion, priests have largely disappeared from the landscape. But the need for the priestly functions that these people carried out for so long have not disappeared: we still require people to help us understand the strange events of our lives, to help us acknowledge our own brokenness, to encourage us to be kinder, more open and more forgiving around others, to advise us around difficult problems, to engage with our grief and to help us find transcendence.

Some of the traditional roles of the priest have passed on to the figure of the psychotherapist. The psychotherapist, like the priest, listens to our sorrows, helps us to make sense of our lives and meets the loneliest and most disturbed parts of our secret selves.

Like the priest, the therapist tries to make us feel safe enough to look honestly at the least likeable and awkward parts of who we are. They try sympathetically to help us understand how we came to be like this; they invite us to greater self-compassion and hence also to compassion for others who are, in their own way, as broken as we are. And they try to identify the steps we can realistically take to limit the damage we inflict on ourselves and others.

The therapist is not specifically interested in the worldly accomplishment of a client who comes to see them. To the therapist this person is defined much more by their inner life. A therapeutic session might pay immense attention to a dispute about some small detail of domestic life, while a major deal that is at stake in the office doesn't get mentioned. In particular therapy is engaged in trying to understand, and lessen the intensity, of our typical belief that we need to be special in order to be loved.

Most of all, therapists take on the role of a confessor. They know that unburdening ourselves on a regular basis, speaking candidly of our most peculiar, dangerous, pathetic or terrifying thoughts is among life's most redemptive activities.

In a better world, there would be places in every city and village, on the high street and in prominent buildings, where – at modest cost and with little fuss – we would be able to go and escape our normal responsibilities in order to sit quietly with a kindly person and tell them everything: the bad stuff we'd done, and even more of the bad stuff we'd thought of doing. We'd talk of sex, of course, but also of envy, meanness and indifference, of failures of courage and of wildly idealistic hopes of change. We'd explain that we wanted to sleep with our partner's sister and with someone entirely inappropriate at work. We'd confess we'd been turned on by a very forbidden person at the library and looked in a way we shouldn't at the swimming pool. We'd reveal we'd been tempted to leave our family or to quit our jobs. We'd say we were entirely fed up and sad, and sometimes just wanted to lie in a ball and cry. We'd confess to the sorts of things that, if they were published in a newspaper, would get us laughed at, humiliated and excluded forever from polite society – and we'd feel so good after doing so, it would teach us that trying to live by the morality of the newspaper is part of what makes us so ill in the first place.

And when we were done, our friendly confessor would simply look at us with infinite kindness and sympathy and say, *I understand*. Our confessor would be unshockable – they'd have a deep understanding of the wellsprings of human insanity, combined with enormous tenderness and generosity of spirit. They would know how crazy we all can be without thereby forfeiting our right to exist.

Many of us are still so hostile to religion for its flaws that we overlook how ingenious some elements are. The little booth, the regularity, the anonymity, the awareness that we get sick from keeping too much in, the importance of allowing people a chance to out themselves and improve in an atmosphere of love; all this the priests understood – and we've largely forgotten.

When every last argument has been angrily made about why therapy doesn't 'work', it remains that for the price of a meal for two, we can tell a therapist every last murderous, incestuous, unacceptable, humiliating, tragic thought and be met with only sympathy, acceptance and curiosity. It can be, quite literally, lifesaving.

Very few of us are properly bad people, but many of us feel like very bad people and have certainly done and thought some pretty odd things. But we are not, on that score, abnormal or beyond forgiveness, redemption and understanding. We are just operating with an overly narrow concept of normality and a desperately punitive idea of what is permissible.

It may not always be easy to find the right therapist. But we need regular occasions for confession, for we will otherwise suffocate from all the secrets inside us and from the fear of being judged and condemned. We need the opportunity to let another human being know the complex, peculiar and sometimes desperately unimpressive reality involved in being us.

In carrying out their functions, there were key advantages that the priest of the past had over today's therapist. In the language of business, we could say that religions industrialised the priestly function. The religion would identify certain core tasks and then employ large numbers of people to carry them out in standard ways. Any one priest was part of a wide network whose labour was reinforced by that of his colleagues. By contrast, today, a psychotherapist is essentially a self-employed individual. However well their individual practice goes, it will almost inevitably be limited to what they personally can achieve. Psychotherapy is a cottage industry.

Another problem is to do with branding. In their heyday, priests had immense prestige. This didn't derive from their own individual merits so much as from their position in large and evidently impressive organisations. In the 16th century, for instance, the Catholic church in Europe systematically built up its brand via immense investments in art, architecture and music. It was harder to ignore what a priest was saying when he was backed up by more or less all the great creative figures of his era. In 18th century England, the Anglican brand was deliberately constructed around ties to the British monarchy and to the major universities. It meant that when the local priest was making a point, they weren't just speaking for themselves: they were standing as representatives of an organisation of undeniable significance.

By contrast, at present, the prestige of therapy and of individual therapists is dismally low. It's not the fault of what they are saying and doing – it's rather that their role isn't backed up by a large and impressive brand that can transmit a collective prestige to them as individuals. And so the function of therapy remains largely invisible to the wider world and the therapist has nothing to rely on except the authority that they can individually win for themselves and which will disappear at their death.

We believe that therapy is the modern inheritor of an all-important range of priestly functions – released from their dependence on speculative faith in other-worldly beings.

But in order to perform these functions with greater authority and reach, therapy needs to take on lessons from religion. It needs to learn the art of organisation, in which the efforts of individual therapists are conjoined and harmonised. And it needs to construct a brand that can make what it stands for properly visible in a deeply inattentive and crowded modern world. We should, as a result, be a little slower always to call first for the doctor.

✳

VIII.

COMMUNITY

✳

Although our societies have, in theory, a very high regard for the idea of community, it is telling that, in practice, 'community centres' are often the most uninspiring and unlovely of all buildings. They can be architecturally very undistinguished, they may have been vandalised and not patched up properly, they can be home to desperate or intimidating figures – and they may offer little for people who don't have an interest in table tennis, bingo or snooker.

By being less than inspiring, our current community centres unwittingly imply that there must be some form of conflict between an investment in 'community' and our deeper hopes for fulfilment for ourselves. Instead of countering individualism, the centres may paradoxically spur on more private forms of ambition, hinting that the drive for personal success should be paramount, for we might otherwise have no option but to spend our days in compromised surroundings. Rather than bolstering community, these centres whisper to us that communal enthusiasm would be something to lean on only when other, better hopes had already failed.

Whatever their many doctrinal and institutional flaws, religions have been experts at building a properly inspiring sense of community. Even those who lack any interest in the faith-based aspects of religion tend to feel a degree of respect, even nostalgia, for the way in which religions have attenuated loneliness, brought together people from very different walks of life and framed the idea of being in a group in the most dignified and ambitious terms.

The example of religions opens up a richer sense of what community could be – and in particular, and very concretely, it offers us a set of ideas about how we might go about constructing new kinds of community centres, which would capture the highest hopes for a more collective way of life.

I. OUTSTANDING BUILDINGS

The great religions have in general spared no expense in building their community centres. For many centuries, these centres – temples, mosques, synagogues, churches and cathedrals – were simply the most impressive structures in existence, whether private or public. Nothing could rival them in magnificence, grace and intelligence. To walk underneath their high-beamed ceilings, carved colonnades or painted porticoes was to feel awed and moved by the majesty that underpinned them.

The Golden Temple, Kyoto, originally completed 1397

One's home might be very comfortable and in its own way accomplished, but it could never be as visually delightful as the centres of communal worship. The finest architects would compete to work on them, the pride of a whole society would be directed towards them and the wealthy would be largely unresentful about helping to pay for them. There was, the architecture hinted, to be no conflict between the demands of the individual ego and collective pride. Dominating the skyline of premodern cities, the religious community centres proclaimed the superlative importance of collective life.

Any attempt to build on the legacy of religions would have to begin with similarly outstanding architecture; the community centres of the future would need to be unquestionably among the most attractive buildings in their districts. Rather than utilitarian sheds put up with maximal economy and minimal inspiration, they would need to leave users astonished at their refinement, comfort and artistry and different neighbourhoods would engage in the healthiest kind of competition to ensure that theirs stood out among rivals. There would have to be pretty much nowhere else a person with options would rather spend their time in.

II. INTRODUCTIONS

Religions have always taken care not just to bring us together, but also to introduce us to one another. They have sensed our otherwise dominant proclivity to stand next to people without ever opening our hearts to them, to inhabit the same space for a while but never to reveal our humanity. This explains why, at the start of a Catholic mass, priests (or to give them their proper and telling designation, 'hosts') encourage the congregation to turn left and right and share a blessing with their neighbours (and perhaps later invite them for refreshments in the garden), or why at the festival of Purim, rabbis will suggest that the entire community drink and eat together in an atmosphere of sympathy and kindness. In the Zen Buddhist tea ceremony, the tea master or mistress will suggest conversation topics for the assembled company and steer them towards themes of sincerity and meaning.

The modern secular world is not without a theoretical interest in communal spaces. Our cities abound in bars, clubs, cinemas and theatres. But what is striking is that such locations almost never facilitate meetings between people. They bring us together without helping us to throw off the inhibitions which hold us back from speaking (at least with any degree of honesty and profundity) to strangers. We eat together in large restaurants but remain anonymous to all but the select group of individuals we came in with. We watch the same plays or films, but without any opportunity to share our emotions with those around us. We wander the cavernous halls of museums, carefully pretending that we are entirely alone.

The community centres of the future would take care to ensure that community is not simply a concept or an aspiration, but a lived reality. They would frame the rules of how we interact in their spaces – and insist that, once we were over the threshold, anyone could be approached without fear of intrusion or judgement. They would help us to feel that we were in a zone of safety and kindness and they would give us tools and rituals with which to express our desire for mutual support and self-revelation. There would be shared meals and special moments where (see Chapter X: Rituals) we would be able to ask questions with which to lever open our shyer, deeper selves. We would no longer be just physically together but also, an infinitely trickier yet more important proposition, psychologically together as well.

III. A GATHERING OF EQUALS

At most gatherings in the secular world, the most common enquiry we field is around what we 'do' and, according to how impressive our answer is, we will either be welcomed and feted or silently abandoned and ignored. The currencies of the social world are overwhelmingly financial and professional. No one is especially interested in whether we happen to be kind or nice.

It is this set of worldly priorities that religions have traditionally subverted in their community centres. Zen Buddhism insisted that all nobles leave their weapons (richly decorated markers of status) at the entrance of tea halls. At Friday prayers, Muslim congregations would deliberately mix up their members, so that a mule driver might be kneeling besides a doctor.

The community centres of the future would, in an analogous way, work at foregrounding a value system that differed from the dominant one in the world beyond their doors. What would count would be sincerity, kindness, imagination and a commitment to emotional connection. It would – for a little while – no longer matter so much 'what one did', so long as one knew how to acknowledge vulnerability and invest in fellowship.

IV. BEYOND SNOOKER

Modern communal spaces tend to gather us together in order to eat, shop and watch or play sport. These may be important priorities at points, but they are only the start of what we might want or need to do while around other people.

What distinguished religions was that their community centres were places where one could perform psychological activities as opposed to merely material ones. Here one could – in the company of others – express one's sorrows, celebrate beauty, give voice to longings for transcendence and offer and receive sympathy. Psychological needs were not relegated (as the secular realm now encourages) to so-called private life. Meaningful moments were not reserved for the home and relationships between couples or parents and their children. One's heart might be touched to the core in a vast crowd.

In Catholic churches, even confessional boxes were placed in public view. The boxes might give privacy, but they were themselves conspicuous, signalling that an admission of our brokenness wasn't shameful or strange – but was an admirable and noble act that everyone should regularly partake in.

Ornate confessionals in which
to share your deepest secrets.

In the community centres of the future, we wouldn't merely be invited to swim and play badminton together, but also – at points – to have psychotherapy in beautifully designed adjoining booths.

V. BEYOND THE NEWS

Religious buildings of old were, by their nature, in touch with the transcendent themes of existence: here, one would gather to remember the lessons of someone who lived a thousand years before, or dwelt high in the heavens above. One's mind would be drawn away from the concerns of the present moment by the sight of graves in the grounds outside or by plaques and scrolls detailing weddings and births from long ago. The grand language, the light filtering in from a distant oculus and the relative quiet or background sound of water would all serve to still the mind and clear away its pettier present obsessions.

A visit to a community centre of the future should likewise broaden our psychological horizons, separating us from the concerns of the media-driven present and reconnecting us with time past and time future. The building would contain memorials to individual and collective tragedies and joys: a son lost at sea, a wedding ten summers before. The more resonant dimensions of existence would be kept in view and set up as worthy subjects of contemplation. The precise and often dismaying details of our own lives would matter less; we would be released from an ordinary preoccupation with ourselves – and immersed in the great cyclical truths.

—

Our societies are infinitely richer than those that built the great community centres of old. But our imaginations are – insofar as an interest in what is collective is concerned – a great deal more limited. We know how to build communal sports facilities, shopping centres, libraries and schools, but we are as yet unsure of how to give public expression to a yet more significant longing in us: to make ourselves at home in the world and to open our hearts not only to kin (family), but also – to use a word that has almost dropped out of our vocabulary – to kith (acquaintances, neighbours, associates) as well.

＊

IX

SAINTS

✳

Religions have been interested in helping us to become better people. At the same time, they have recognised that we learn to grow wise not so much by reading abstract essays about the ingredients of wisdom but by studying wise lives. We improve through proximity to conspicuously kind, humane, thoughtful and gentle people. We need – to reach our full potential – to have the right role models around us.

The modern world is not devoid of people we might model ourselves on. They normally go by the name of celebrities. Typically, celebrity attaches itself to people who have had very conspicuous success in singing, acting, commerce or professional sport. The tricky thing is that the accomplishments of these people don't necessarily correspond very intimately with the issues we actually have to face in our own lives. The qualities that make them so prominent – their remarkable good looks, their physical prowess, their relentless competitive instincts, their perfectionism – are ones we can't easily share or learn from; and being continually exposed to them can reinforce a sense of our own comparative inadequacy. At the same time, modern celebrity cruelly feeds the idea that, in order to have a good life, we need to be famous, a woeful implication because we're extremely unlikely ever to become prominent and because, in any case, being known to very large numbers of strangers has no connection to personal happiness and is indeed generally a sure route to mental sickness.

It could be tempting to draw the conclusion that in a better society we'd not have celebrities. But the history of religion points to another possibility. Religions were very interested in making certain people famous: they just had a very different picture of what sorts of people should be known and how they could benefit the rest of us by being so.

A particularly ambitious theory of celebrity – the saints – was developed by Catholicism. A saint was a person who was systematically to be brought to public attention because they possessed to an unusual degree a psychological quality deemed to be universally relevant in living a good life. Francis of Assisi became a celebrity because he knew how to be modest, kind and devoid of pomposity. A woman called Theresa, from the town of Avila in Spain, became a saint because she was very patient and tactful with her sometimes annoying colleagues, while also being admirably focused on efficiency in her work with the disadvantaged. Philip Neri's celebrity was based on the fact that he was a highly humane administrator of schools and hospitals. There was an important additional qualification for this kind of religious celebrity: a self-conscious desire to be a saint automatically disqualified a person from being one.

Having identified an individual as a saint, the Church would then systematically promote their fame by commissioning statues and paintings of them, by referring to their life story in songs and sermons and by assigning a day of the year to their memory.

Fra Angelico, *The Forerunners of Christ with Saints and Martyrs*, c.1423–1424

In attempting to replace religion, we can productively build on and revise the idea of the saint. In the secular world too, we would benefit from foregrounding certain people, who could encapsulate, with particular clarity, qualities that we need to thrive and endure. These exemplary people would not in any way need to be perfect (indeed, it would be by allowing us to witness their imperfections that we could grow more tolerant of our own) – they wouldn't need to know how to sing, model clothes or take part in action films. They might be leading quite ordinary lives, they might not be too beautiful, thin, educated or young – and yet they would be gifted in certain areas of psychology in ways that could provide us with vital inspiration for meeting the challenges of our lives. We'd see documentaries about them, there might be books and photographs of them, we'd learn their names, subtly pick up their lessons – and wonder what they might advise us to think or do at points of particular crisis.

In pulling together a family of modern 'saints', we would be looking for people with some of the following qualities.

I. BROKENNESS

We would need someone with a native genius for admitting their own failings and flaws, without giving way to bitterness or defensiveness. They would take the business of laughing at themselves seriously. They would hedge their pronouncements, they would be sceptical in their conclusions and would gently laugh at the constant collisions between the noble way they would have liked things to be and the demented way they in fact so often turn out. They would have come to terms with their tendencies to idiocy, ugliness and error, but would not be fundamentally ashamed of themselves because they had already shed so much of their pride.

II. MELANCHOLIA UNIVERSALIS

Here we would need people who knew how to be gratifyingly modest about the chances of anything turning out too well. They would be 'realistic' about how challenging many things can be. They would be fully conscious of the complexities entailed in any project: for example, raising a child, starting a business, spending an agreeable weekend with the family, changing the nation, falling in love ... Knowing that something difficult was being attempted wouldn't rob them of ambition, but it would make them more steadfast, calmer and less prone to panic about the problems that would invariably come their way. They would rarely expect anything to be wholly easy or to go entirely well. At times, they would know how to give way to sorrow publicly. They would be both strong and wholly at home with their weakness and grief. Their prominent place in our culture would make us all more confident about honouring our darker, sadder states of mind.

DEPENDENCE

We would need someone who could confidently foreground their reliance on others, who was proud of being a small part of a larger team and who, though very much an adult, would regularly think of those who brought them to maturity. We would sense their admiration for people who made their community, workplace or group what it is and note how unimportant it was for them to take too much of the credit for collective acts. They might put particular emphasis on their hobbies and not neglect interests of theirs which didn't attract money or status. Such an individual would be a living antidote to the powerful, but unfortunate, idea that we must always be self-made and that our identity must be constructed around our own worldly achievements alone. They would help us see what might be charming and reassuring about dependence.

III. ORDINARY LIFE

A potential saint in this area would be living a so-called quiet life, away from the obvious centres of glamour and prestige, and yet would still know how to imbue their actions and surroundings with dignity, intelligence and seriousness. They would be unusually alive to moments of calm and beauty, even extremely modest ones, of the kind that those with grander plans rush past. With the dangers and tragedies of existence firmly in mind, they would take pleasure in a single, uneventful, sunny day, or some pretty flowers growing by a brick wall, the charm of a three-year-old playing in a garden or an evening of intimate conversation among friends. It isn't that they would be sentimental and naive – precisely the opposite: because they would know how hard things can get, they would draw the full value from the peaceful and the sweet, in however humble a form these might arise.

IV. TRAGEDY

Here we would be on the lookout for an individual who was accomplished, good and talented and yet had met with an undue amount of failure and disappointment, on the basis of a small and very forgivable error. They would clearly be decent people who had tried hard, and we would wince at the price they had to pay for their mistakes. Their task would be to remind us that the link between merit and reward can be appallingly weak and unreliable.

V. TRANSCENDENCE

A strong candidate here would know that all human beings, themselves included, are never far from folly: they have irrational desires and incompatible aims, they are unaware of a lot of what they feel, they are prone to mood swings, they are visited by powerful fantasies and delusions – and are always buffeted by the curious demands of their sexuality. A saint in this area would look down at the mad human spectacle as if from outer space and would be unsurprised by the ongoing co-existence of deep immaturity and perversity alongside quite adult qualities like intelligence and morality. They would know (without bitterness) that we are barely evolved apes. Aware that at least half of life is irrational, they would try – wherever possible – to budget for madness and would be slow to panic when it (reliably) reared its head. They might, in their professional lives, be working in an observatory.

VI. GOOD ENOUGH

Here we would find a person who is both fully aware of the compromises and tensions of long-term love and committed to trying to find a decent way through them with humour and tenderness. They would have overcome their earlier Romanticism and could accept without impatience or bitterness that their partner could not be everything to them and vice versa, but that the union was, nevertheless, in significant ways, 'good enough.' They would not leap to the worst conclusions about what was going on in the minds of their partners. They would be readier to overlook a slight from a proper sense of how difficult every life is – harbouring as it does so many frustrated ambitions, disappointments and longings. They would be generous to the reasons for which their partners in particular, and people in general, might not always behave nicely. They would feel less persecuted by the aggression and meanness of others because they would have a due sense of where their hurt tends to come from. Their example would help to move us away from our own persecutory perfectionism.

VII. RECURRENCE

Here we would be looking for someone who was perhaps very old, but still sprightly of spirit and unshocked by life. They might have worked for many years in a maternity ward or on the stock exchange. They would have seen so many crises and have lived through much that was far worse than the present moment. They would, at points, be usefully unexcited by what was happening right now, because they would see it in a larger perspective against which it would lose its unwarranted drama. They might also be very responsive to nature, perhaps knowing everything about the eating habits of a badger or the cycles of the moons of Jupiter. They would see human life within a larger framework of nature, history and space – and therefore interpret it as something a great deal less special and less alarming than it often appears on the evening news.

A replacement for religion would continually promote individuals such as these. As with current celebrities, they'd turn up regularly in the press, we'd frequently be getting updates on what they happened to be doing and would often encounter their point of view in magazines and books. They'd be a focus of collective reference: everyone would have heard of them and have a sense of what they stood for. Via their examples, we'd be repeatedly meeting the core consoling ideas we needed and would be granted an image of what we ourselves might want to be a bit more like one day – once we had grown a little wiser and more mature.

*

X.

RITUALS

✳

I. INTRODUCTION

The concept of ritual has a habit of sounding either unappealing or plain weird to modern ears. We don't much like the idea of having to submit to old-fashioned rules; to say certain, perhaps quite formal-sounding, things; or to join in with a group at a prescribed time and go through unusual rites. The modern world was founded on the notion of being able to feel things our way, at a time of our choosing, and to be as casual and informal as we like. Correspondingly, we assume there could be nothing more ridiculous than repeating an old idea again and again. Repetition sounds boring and irksome: like the worst experiences of childhood education.

But religions have taken a very different view. They have been profoundly interested in ritual. They have created aesthetically seductive occasions, where certain lessons are rehearsed and emphasised. Zen Buddhists have looked at the moon ritualistically every autumn and written poems in its honour on a set day; Jews take time to appreciate spring according to a ritual requirement of their holy calendar; Catholics are required to ritually examine their consciences every Sunday; in Russia, Orthodox ritual demanded that before a long journey, everyone would meditate briefly on the possibility of never seeing each other again.

What fired the religious devotion to ritual was the realisation that if the goal was to change minds and behaviour (and thereby change the world), doing something once, in an informal and ad hoc way, was never going to be enough.

In a secular age, the deep link between religion and ritual has served to cast the very concept of ritual into shadow. This is unfair. The most important ideas should keep being reinforced via aesthetically compelling rituals. On a regular basis we should be reminded of the importance of concepts like brokenness, melancholy, dependence or tragedy. We may not disagree with such ideas but, without rituals, we will simply forget to act upon them in practice. We need rituals to ensure that we properly listen to the significance of what we half-know already, but avoid ever properly putting into practice nevertheless.

Rituals reject the notion that it can ever be sufficient to teach anything important once – an optimistic delusion which the modern education system has been fatefully marked by. Once might be enough to get us to admit an idea is right, but it won't be anything like enough to convince us it should be acted upon. Our brains are leaky and, under pressure of any kind, they will readily revert to customary patterns of thought and feeling. Rituals train our cognitive muscles, they make a sequence of appointments in our diaries to refresh our acquaintance with our most important ideas.

Our current culture tends to see ritual mainly as an antiquated infringement of individual freedom, a bossy command to turn our thoughts in particular directions at specific times. But the defenders of ritual would see it another way: we aren't being told to think of something we don't agree with, we are being returned with grace to what we always believed in at heart. We are being tugged by a collective force back to a more loyal and authentic version of ourselves.

Religions have always wanted to do something much more serious than simply promote abstract ideas – they have wanted to get people to behave in line with those ideas, which is a very different thing. They didn't just want people to think kindness or forgiveness were nice (which generally we do already) – they wanted us to be kind or forgiving most days of the year. That meant inventing a host of ingenious mechanisms for mobilising the will, which is why, across much of the world, the finest art and buildings, the most seductive music, the most impressive and moving rituals have all been religious. Religion is a vast machine for addressing our forgetful minds.

The challenge for the secular world is now to redevelop its own rituals – so that we will cease so regularly to ignore our real commitments and might henceforth not only believe wise things but also, on a day-to-day basis, have a slightly higher chance of enacting wisdom in our lives.

The essence of rituals is an attempt to mark out an event from the flow of ordinary life. At moments of ritual, we might wear clothes that are a bit more formal than usual or speak in ways that are a bit unlike ordinary conversation – all so as to isolate what is happening from ordinary events.

There is, in modern times, an understandable keenness to reduce the oddity of rituals, to get the participants to speak more colloquially, to wear everyday clothes and to behave as they might in a kitchen. But this is to misunderstand some of the point of rituals. There are occasions and events that should be trying to mark a break from normal routines, to take us out of normal time and put us in touch with something very special.

The School of Life proposes five major rituals:

THE CREDO

A ritual in which a group of people repeat together, in a service that can incorporate music, readings, films and talks, eight central tenets that console and protect us against some of the challenges of contemporary life.

1   BROKENNESS

We are inherently flawed and broken beings.

Perfection is beyond us.

Despite our intelligence and our science, we will never stamp out stupidity and pain. Life will always continue to be – in central ways – about suffering.

We are all, from close up, scared, unsure, full of regret, longing and error.

We are not unusual in our follies. The only people we can think of as 'normal' are those we don't yet know very well.

Recognition of our inherent madness, weakness and error should not be a source of shame. From it flows compassion for ourselves and generosity towards others.

Knowing how to reveal our vulnerability and brokenness is the beginning of compassion and friendship.

2   MELANCHOLIA UNIVERSALIS

We are under undue and unfair pressure to smile.

But grief is our more natural, and more consoling home.

Nothing good will be easy or go entirely well:
We can expect frustration, misunderstanding,
misfortune and rebuffs.

Though there is a vast amount to feel sad about
We're not individually cursed.

Against the backdrop of sorrow
The small sweet things stand out:
A sunny day, a drifting cloud;
Dawn and dusk,
A tender look ...

We can believe in cheerful despair.

3   DEPENDENCE

We did not make ourselves unaided.
We are dependent creatures.
We're loyal to a bigger understanding of our lives.

From the start, as children
We needed the kindness and help of others
And we still do.
We need the mercy of a second chance,
We need encouragement,
We need forgiveness because none of us
Can stand the severest truths of who we are and
what we've done.

We can take pride in belonging to things bigger
that ourselves.
We can love what we belong to
Though it doesn't just belong to us.
We can be proud of what others have done for us
And not only of what we've done for ourselves.

4   ORDINARY LIFE

We are not heroes; we recognise ourselves as
ordinary
And are committed to seeing the merits of our
ordinary lives.

We see what is lovely, sweet, good and important
About simple and commonplace things.
'Ordinary' isn't a name for failure.
Understood more carefully,
And seen with a more generous and perceptive
eye,
It contains the best of life.

Life is not elsewhere; is it, fully and properly,
Here and now.

5   TRAGEDY

People do not reliably end up with the lives they
deserve.
There is no real justice in the way that rewards are
distributed.
We are subject to appalling whims of chance and
ill luck.

We should embrace the idea of tragedy.
We see that terrible things can and do befall lives.

A small mistake, a minor flaw can lead to horror:
Someone like us could be bankrupt, in jail or
vilified in the press.

We can fail and be good;
All the tragedies of others live in embryo in us.

We need to be slower to judge and quicker to
understand.
Those who have failed are not 'losers'.
We may soon be among them.

6   TRANSCENDENCE

We are not at the centre of anything; thankfully.
We are minuscule bundles of matter on an
infinitesimal corner of a boundless universe.
We do not count, in the grander scheme.

We need the relief of a cosmos that doesn't care –
The kindly indifference of infinity:
An eternity where no one will notice
Where the wind erodes the rocks,
In the space between the stars.

Silence and humility are a blessing
After a life of jostling and anxious pride.

7   GOOD ENOUGH

Anyone we could love would frustrate us
profoundly over time.
True love isn't about admiring perfection; it is
about being charitable to what is weak and broken.

A feeling of compatibility should not be a
precondition of love;
It is its consequence.

We will at points wish our partners dead and think
the day we met them the worst of our lives.
And at other points, we will recognise them as
being very much good enough.

'The one' is a cruel invention.
No one is ever 'right'. But being a little wrong isn't
the end of anything;
It's the only true basis upon which lasting love can
be built.

8   RECURRENCE

We get transfixed by the new
But most of life has happened before:
The giant wheel keeps turning.

Love is difficult,
Work is hard,
Societies are mad,
Politics goes wrong,
No one is loved as much as they deserve,
Everyone is lonely and afraid;
There's nothing weirder than being alive –
Then we sicken and we die.

The more we concentrate
On novelty
The harder it is to hear the vital things
Which may have happened long ago.

We need a culture that can remind us
Often enough
And in ways we can bear to hear
Of the older things we very much still need to
know.

THE SCHOOL DINNER

The School of Life's School Dinner is a ritual that unfolds, ideally, once a year, among a group of friends. By sharing this ritual experience, we grow less isolated, ashamed and afraid. Witnessing ideas being taken seriously by others strengthens our own trust in them.

The School Dinner is divided into eight distinct stages, each of which combines a small lesson with something to eat or drink. One person, the Director, should take it upon themselves to read the text that follows and to guide the other participants at relevant moments.

The meal begins. The table has been carefully and elegantly laid. There might be candles and flowers. Participants have made an effort with their clothes.

1   THE MOMENT OF HUMAN BROKENNESS

The director   A primary obstacle to our individual and collective tranquillity is the belief that people can be perfect. We continually imagine others to be much more coherent and fortunate than we are. Considering them only from the outside, we picture them as sharing few of our deep anxieties and regrets. In company, we back away from admission of our own fears and failings, out of dread of ridicule and shame. And yet, in a fiendish irony, others are inside almost certainly as mournful and isolated as we are.

A plate of walnuts is passed around, people crack them open (with some difficulty). The shared acknowledgement of our brokenness and foolishness is symbolised by the ritual eating of this nut, a symbol of the inherent faultiness of our minds.

The director Acknowledgement of our natural brokenness isn't a way of humiliating ourselves: it's a relief from an excessive cultural investment in the idea of progress and perfection and in the attendant desire to blame people (especially ourselves) when we fail – as we inevitably will.

2 THE MOMENT OF CONFESSION

Before the meal, each guest has been asked to write down on a small piece of paper something very intimate that they feel sad about, something they are worried might happen, or an area of their life in which they are lonely or misunderstood. They write something about what makes them feel guilty, what they are ashamed of and disgusted by. Importantly, this is a confession – not an attempt to pin the blame on anyone else. The pieces of paper are entirely anonymous. Everyone comes to the meal with a confession slip in their bag or pocket.

At the end of the starter, the Director takes a large bowl and asks all the guests to put their pieces of paper into it. The results are mixed so that their authors cannot be identified.

The director We've each made a specific admission of our troubles and brokenness: individually, we've taken a risk because these are the things about us that we take such care to keep out of sight – out of natural anxiety about what others will think of us. But here we're confessing together, for we are among friends. The vulnerability we expose isn't one-sided: it's matched by the vulnerability of everyone else. The single greatest cure for the wretchedness of our collective condition is to know that we are not alone in suffering. We can reveal, because others have revealed. Our confessions don't isolate us, they are our entry ticket into a consoling community.

Someone at the other end of the table reads out a selection of the confessions at random.

3   THE MOMENT OF CONSOLATION

In this part of the ritual, we acknowledge the presence of a child in each one of us.

The director   When we grow physically, when we take up an adult position in the world, we are still in many ways like children. To recall the child means adopting the charitable, patient, forgiving and warm attitude we instinctively adopt towards a distressed three-year-old.

While we eat, we should go around the table and each person should describe, in some detail, what it was like for them to be a child: what were they excited by, what troubled them, what made them sad or frightened, what and who they loved. The consolation comes from seeing ourselves collectively in a more generous light: we are all still these small people, still deeply connected emotionally to who we were when we were vulnerable and endearing.

4 THE MOMENT OF THE SURRENDER OF HOPE

After the main course, and before the dessert, there is a moment when we are invited to write down, on another small piece of paper, a longing that we've been nurturing – perhaps for a long time – in our imaginations. Maybe we dream one day of making a fortune; perhaps we hope to rise to the top of our profession; we might long to find the ideal partner; we might hope that our child will forgive us; or that we'll be properly reconciled with a parent.

The diners read out a selection of their hopes.

The director

These are beautiful ideals. But they have a tragic dimension: however much we long for them, they are unlikely to come true. Our hopes and intentions are weak twigs in the chaos of the world. Our investment in perfection – in getting precisely what we long for – does not make this outcome more likely. It sets us up for appalling frustration and resentment.

The hopes are surrendered. The Director either lights the pieces of paper on which they are written (if this can be done safely) or very publicly disposes of them in a bin.

The director

This moment symbolises the public abandonment of hopes that have for too long tortured us. It's a cathartic occasion as we see not just our grand hopes, but those of everyone else, being renounced. We can face sorrow, when it is presented not as an unusual punishment, but as the normal fate of everyone on the planet.

5   THE MOMENT OF MELANCHOLIA
     UNIVERSALIS

*Shortly before the dessert is served, an empty bowl is
placed upon the table: ideally it is rustic and plain.*

The director   Melancholy is a central human experience: it is not
an illness that needs to be cured or a sign of any
special kind of failure. Melancholy is sorrow that
isn't connected to anger or blame. It is a tender,
generous and honest admission of the centrality
of suffering in human experience. Normally,
melancholy is deeply private, but now we know
everyone is feeling something similar. We don't
need to say anything. For a minute, let us each
experience our own sadness in the company of
others.

6   THE MOMENT OF APPRECIATION

The director   We've abandoned certain dreams. We have paused
to recognise the melancholy nature of the human
condition. What remains?

*On the tables, dishes have arrived bearing figs on the
one hand, and small pieces of dark chocolate on the
other.*

The director   We are left with small pleasures. The standard
habit of the mind is to take careful note what's
not right in our lives and obsess about all that is
missing. But we can also pause and notice some
of what has, remarkably, not gone wrong. We can
take delight in the fig, a symbol of wisdom, and
in dark chocolate, a symbol of self-love. Against a

backdrop of acknowledged sadness, 'small things' can seem larger than we might have supposed; no longer a petty distraction from a mighty destiny or an insult to ambition, but a genuine pleasure amidst a litany of troubles, an invitation to bracket anxieties and keep self-criticism at bay, a small resting place for hope in a sea of disappointment.

Thereafter, we go round the table and each person in turn identifies a small pleasure that they are particularly taken by.

The director

Ironically it's sometimes only when the big lights of our grand hopes are turned off that we can see the smaller, but perfectly real, lights of our everyday satisfactions.

7 THE MOMENT OF SANE INSANITY

Chamomile tea is served.

The director

None of us can be wholly sane. What we should aim for is therefore a knowledgeable and self-possessed relationship to our manifold insanities, or what we might term 'sane insanity.' The sane-insane differ from the simply insane by virtue of the honest and accurate grasp they have on what is not entirely right with them. They may not be wholly balanced, but they don't have the additional folly of insisting on their normalcy.

They can admit with good grace – and no particular loss of dignity – that of course they are rather peculiar at a myriad of points. They warn others as far as possible in advance of what being around them might involve – and apologise promptly for their failings as soon as they have manifested themselves. They offer their friends and companions accurate maps to their craziness, which is about the most generous thing one can do to anyone who has to endure us. The sane-insane among us are not a special category of the mentally unwell: we represent the most evolved possibility for a mature human being.

As we drink a cup of tea, towards the close of the ritual meal, we go around the table and each person admits some way in which they are crazy and a burden to others.

8 THE FINAL MOMENT: CHEERFUL DESPAIR

The ritual School Dinner closes with a moment in which, as we separate, we wish each other 'cheerful despair'. It sounds paradoxical of course. Normally we see cheerfulness and despair as directly opposed states of mind: either you are in one or the other.

The director

Cheerful despair grows from an acceptance of the bleak nature of the human condition: we are living on a dunghill of folly, greed, injustice, error and arrogance. Our lives are brief and filled with suffering. But if we properly admit that this is how things normally are, we won't read our circumstances with special resentment or anger. We're starting out from the assumption that deception, indifference, deviance, boasting, ignorance and selfishness are entirely normal facets of the human character. We're not shocked or outraged when we meet them on a regular basis. Strangely – but importantly – it is from this starting assumption that cheerfulness and gratitude finally have a chance to thrive.

As we shake hands or exchange a kiss on the cheek we murmur to each other the essential words: 'cheerful despair'.

THE GATHERING

In order to remind ourselves of our mutual dependence and comforting brokenness, these are ritual occasions, that take place once in a month, in which strangers and friends gather and ask each other the following questions in a spirit of friendship, genuine enquiry, deep listening and radical honesty.

January

AMBITION

- Were your parents fulfilled in their ambitions for themselves?

- What were your parents' ambitions for you?

- What remains for you to achieve?

- Who would you like to impress?

- What achievements of others make you jealous?

- What personal vulnerabilities and flaws have held you back in your ambitions?

- What, for you, is the relationship between lovability and achievement?

- What is failure for you?

- What alternative careers do you suspect you might be rather good at?

- What price have you paid for your ambitions?

- What is the best way to cope with the disapproval or neglect of the world?

- Knowing what you now know, how would you advise a very young person about their ambitions?

LOVE

- Finish this sentence: If someone likes me a lot, I start to feel ...

- In what ways are people you are attracted to similar to one or other of your parents?

- On a date, what would you most want to be liked for?

- What kinds of suffering would you want a prospective partner to have experienced in the past?

- In what way is your partner (or an ex) quite annoying?

- List five ways in which you are, after all, quite difficult to live with.

- In what ways are you not a great communicator?

- What's tricky about sex?

- Are you good at breaking up?

- Which of your ex-partners hurt you the most?

- Make a case for why adultery could, sometimes, be excused.

- Which of your flaws would you like to be treated more generously?

SELF-KNOWLEDGE

- How much do you like yourself? What do you attribute this to?

- In what ways are you neurotic (given that we all are)?

- What difficulties did your childhood bequeath you?

 How might people describe you when you are not in the room?

- What do you find difficult to communicate directly?

- In what contexts do you find it hard to trust people?

- What do you characteristically do when you are emotionally hurt?

- In what areas of life would you describe yourself as immature?

- How did your mother leave you feeling about yourself? And your father?

- How do you typically respond to frustration?

- What do you think explains why you personally are more of an introvert – or an extrovert?

- How would you still like to grow emotionally?

THE MEANING OF LIFE

- What problem would you like to solve for other people?

- Name two meaningful moments you have had.

- What is a meaningful conversation to you?

- How has your quest for a meaningful life made relationships and your career more meaningful, but more difficult for you?

- Imagine you have five years left to live. Assume you won't be incapacitated until the moment of death. What would you have the confidence to do – now that your death verdict has been announced – that you might previously have lacked?

- In my relationships, I would have the confidence to ...

- In my friendships, I would have the confidence to...

- In my work, I would have the confidence to …

- With my family, I would have the confidence to …

- What's the greatest unhappiness in your interpersonal life at the moment?

- What transcendent experiences have you had? Where were you? What did they feel like?

- What sort of group could you imagine belonging to? What would it need to be like for you to feel proud to belong?

- What advice would you give to your 19-year-old self? How have you grown since then?

May

SECRETS

- Tell your dinner companion a big secret about yourself.

- How do you secretly hope a friend would describe you at your funeral? Be as specific to your individual character as possible.

- What's the worst thing you've ever done? Name the general area if the specifics are too tricky.

- List three things about a person close to you that secretly annoy you.

- What sort of things have made you envious recently?

- What negative character flaws do you fear – in your worst nightmares – that other people have spotted about you?

- List three (now-guilt-inducing) occasions when you were especially mean to certain people.

- What things would alarm your family if they knew?

- What are some of your most pervasive insecurities?

- What do you worry about in the early hours?

- What do you think is quite odd about you?

- Which of your flaws would you want to be forgiven?

RESOLUTIONS

- What immature side of yourself would you like to work on? (We all have them)

- Describe one thing you would do in the coming twelve months if you were a more confident person.

- If you could not fail, what would be the ideal next move in your career?

- Who are you envious of? What positive bit of their life can you introduce into your own?

- Describe your life in the most boosterish, optimistic way. Then in the darkest, most honest, most pessimistic way.

- How did your parents shape what success and failure mean to you?

- What old ambition can you happily let go, knowing you will never achieve it?

- What can you forgive yourself for? What could you forgive another person you know for?

- Who in your life can you draw supportive energy from to realise an ambition? And who drains your energy – who might you have to let go?

- What small evolutionary steps – a daily practice or good habit – could you undertake to realise an ambition?

If this was the last year of your life, how would your resolution change?

- How do you hope your life will look different in a year's time as a result of a resolution?

FAMILY

- What do you blame your parents for?

- What do you credit your parents for?

- What might a good friend of your parents say

about their inadequacies?

- What did you learn about relationships from your parents? What have you tried to unlearn?

- What was once rather sweet about you?

- What qualities did you possess as a child that you wish you still had more of as an adult?

- Have you ever had an imaginary friend or very favourite soft toy? Describe them.

- What were you especially embarrassed about as a teenager?

- If you had to join someone else's family, what sort would it be (design the ideal one)?

- In what ways are you envious of your siblings? (If you do not have siblings, choose other relations of your own generation.)

- Of the family you spend time with, who brings out your best qualities?

- What three things do you enjoy doing most as a family? And least?

WORK

- If I was more of a success, a/my partner would ...

- If I was more of a failure, a/my partner would ...

- Men secretly feel that successful women are ...

- Women secretly feel that successful men are ...

- Could you respect a partner who earned far less than you? How would you feel if your partner earned far more than you?

- You hear of someone who has died. Which of these are you most impressed to learn about their legacy and why?
a. They made a small contribution to a big project that was genuinely worthwhile.
b. They took honourable risks, quite a few of which didn't work out.
c. They put family before maximising income.
d. They were a supportive colleague and mentor.
e. They helped their partner succeed in their career.

- What is the most cynical thing you could say about your work?

- In what ways is your organisation (a bit) dysfunctional?

- Ideally, my colleagues would be more like me. Discuss.

- The best person I ever worked for/with was so good because ...

- When I was a child and thought about the future; I wanted to be ...

- If life were 400 years long, what careers would

you want to have had?

- My ideal obituary would explain that I ...

CONFESSIONS

- Which of your exes would you like to go back and sleep with?

- What do you wish your partner could forgive you for?

- How has your childhood made you difficult to be around?

- What mistakes would you want to avoid in a future relationship?

- Describe your discovery of masturbation.

- What hang-ups do you have around sex?

- What part of your body do you worry might put a lover off?

- What do you want more of in your sex life – but have difficulty asking for or finding?

- How much do you earn?

- What would you fix in your life with infinite money?

- What salary level for another person starts to

make you feel humiliated at your earnings?

- What is it about your character that hasn't enabled you to make more money?

TABOOS

- Are you dominant or submissive sexually? And in the rest of life?

- Have you ever had an incestuous thought? Who was it about?

- Name three sexual scenarios that especially excite you.

- What experience do you have of impotence – yours or a lover's or a friend's?

- How much money do you have in your bank account?

- What would be the first thing you would do if you won the lottery?

- What do you, perhaps secretly, spend really quite a lot of money on?

- Which of your acquaintances/friends/family members makes you feel inadequate around money?

- When have you acted without 100% integrity?

- Have you ever sabotaged your own success?

- When was the last time you experienced 'Schadenfreude'? Do you dare to admit what triggered it?

- Which close relative do you like the least – and why?

THE BODY

- What about your body is desirable?

- In what ways has your physical appearance affected your personality?

- If you could redesign your body from scratch, what would it look like?

- When you look in the mirror, what's the first thing you check?

- What do you find physically attractive in others?

- Give the person you are talking to a sincere compliment about their physical appearance.

- What repels you in other bodies?

- What clothes interest/excite you, for yourself or others?

- What elements of physically ageing are your most afraid of or upset by?

- What might be the upsides of ageing?

- How have you been ageing recently? What do you notice?

- At the current rate, what might you regret on your deathbed?

UTOPIA

- In a better society, what would people be like? Describe their (psychological) characteristics?

- How would you like to be a better person?

- If you had magical powers to 'improve' two people around you, what would you correct in them?

- What are you oddly, perhaps privately, remarkably utopian about? What do you allow yourself to be idealistic about?

- Design your ideal country: how would it be different from your own?

- In your utopia, what would be banned?

- In your utopia, who or what would be more readily forgiven?

- In the utopia, everyone would try out four very different careers in a working life. What would you pick?

- In your utopia, who would deserve to be treated as a celebrity?

- In the utopia, education is a lifelong endeavour. Schools and universities teach their students not just formal knowledge, but the emotional skills they need to thrive. What subject or lesson could you teach?

- In the utopia, advertising does not promote useless things, but virtues and good causes. What would you like to advertise?

- What can you do to make the world a slightly better place?

THE WEDDING

*A practical reimagining of a traditional wedding
ceremony, where ritual is used to enhance the lessons
required to make a real relationship function and be
'good enough'.*

THE MUSICAL PRELUDE

*As the guests enter the ceremonial space, solemn,
ethereal music is played. It should be loud enough to
encourage meditative silence in the congregation. It is
threshold music: we are leaving the familiar world of
day-to-day concerns; there can be no more gossiping
or cheery chat about parking. The mood is grave and
solemn: something very sombre and serious is about
to unfold.*

*After a few minutes, as the music comes to an end,
the director enters and walks slowly to the platform
and sits facing the congregation. On a small table
close to the director's chair are two small books, two
photographs and two rings; these will play important
roles in the ceremony.*

*The two people who are going to be married are, at
this point, seated well away from the platform and as
far from each other as possible.*

THE INTRODUCTION

The music ceases. The director stands up and says:

The director | A wedding marks the attempt to unite two lives.

Experience makes it clear that a married couple face many problems; people who love and care for one another will fall into conflict over issues large and small; they will struggle to understand one another and they will be irked and dismayed by multiple features of each other's characters.

Over the course of this marriage (as over the course of all marriages), there will be resentments, rows, secrets, sorrows, times of boredom and vales of anxiety.

A good marriage is not one from which troubles are magically absent; it is one in which troubles are faced with insight and generosity.

Love is not simply a feeling. It is a set of skills, including the skill of keeping in mind that our partner's most upsetting characteristics are rooted in their past sufferings and that they are expressions of hurt rather than indifference or viciousness. Love is the skill to forgive the wrongs done to us and the refusal to hoard them up as debts for eventual repayment. Love is the skill of seeing clearly our own flaws and failings – and hence of recognising, with gratitude, the generosity our partner daily displays in remaining beside us. It is the skill of understanding that everyone is deeply imperfect and of recognising, therefore, that we are meeting in our partner the faults of human nature, rather than the exceptional failings of one person.

This wedding ceremony marks a moment of public commitment. We, the congregation, are of supreme importance. We are being asked to hear what ... and ... say to one another today and to hold them to what they have openly asserted before us. There will be troubled times ahead when their own wisdom will fall prey to passion and to error. Our presence is designed to give them the love and the courage required for them to live up to their highest selves.

The couple are invited onto the stage.

They come from different directions, as separate people who are approaching one another. They stand either side of the director, facing the assembled guests.

THE RITUAL OF HUMILITY

The director   Humility is perhaps the most important emotion for the success of a relationship. Humility starts with an ample, accurate and sorrowful recognition of all one's failings. It is filled with apology and modesty. It doesn't pretend that flaws are charming quirks or excusable oddities. It contains an open admission that we wish we were different – and better.

Humility carries a shamed apology: I am genuinely and truly sorry for what and who I can sometimes be.

Humility carries an implication of gratitude: I'm profoundly grateful that – given what I am at points – you are willing to share a life with me.

Humility is not one-sided. Each person is damaged and difficult in different ways. The fate of the marriage hangs upon the willingness of each party to admit with grace, on repeated occasions, their own deep and serious inadequacies.

The director turns to one member of the couple, partner one, and asks: Do you admit that you are a failed, broken human being – not in every way, but in some ways so serious that you will at points be a grave burden to ... ?

Partner one

Yes, I admit this. I am failed and broken.

The director

Do you admit that you can be an extraordinary challenge; that you can be deeply difficult?

Partner one

I admit this.

The director

Before coming here today – freely and openly and after careful reflection – you have listed your failings as you recognise them. You have listed them in this book – your own Book of Imperfections. Would you now, before me, your partner and your guests, read some of what you have stated in your own words?

The director points to two volumes on a small table. They are Books of Imperfection, elegantly bound volumes, clearly designed to be kept for a lifetime. Inside, each partner has written up a detailed list of their own failings, infelicities, quirks, shortfalls of maturity and ugly habits.

Partner one picks up their volume and reads a short extract.

(For example: I acknowledge that I can be rigid and cold; I goad and needle. Sometimes I'd rather make you unhappy than let you see and understand my own sorrow. When I get upset I become harsh and cutting.)

The director thanks the first partner then turns to the second.

The director

Do you admit that you are a failed, broken human being – not in every way, but in some ways so serious that you will at points be a grave burden to ... ?

Partner two

Yes, I admit this. I am failed and broken.

The director

Do you admit that you can be an extraordinary challenge; that you can be deeply difficult?

Partner two

Yes, I admit this.

The director

Before coming here today – freely and openly and after careful reflection – you have listed your failings as you recognise them. You have listed them in this book – your own Book of Imperfections. Would you now, before me, your partner and your guests, read some of what you have stated in your own words?

Partner two reads a short extract from their book.

The director thanks the second partner.

The director asks the couple to exchange books. The first partner gives a copy of their Book of Imperfections to the second partner and says:

The director	I give you this book, in which I have recorded the serious and deep failings of my character – as well as I can understand them at the moment – but knowing there are sure to be others, which may be even worse. As a proof of love and trust, I'm showing you what I know to be terrible about me. These are the broken parts of myself, for which I need forgiveness. I am frightened of, and humbled by, the power this gives you. Yet I still want to marry you and hope you still want to marry me.

The director addresses the second partner, who has just received the book and asks: Do you understand the seriousness of what is written here? |
Partner two	Yes.
The director	Have you read it carefully?
Partner two	Yes.
The director	Will you treat this knowledge with kindness?
Partner two	Yes, I will.
The director	Do you promise not to use this knowledge to embarrass your partner in front of other people?
Partner two	Yes.
The director	There may be more faults to come. Can you live with them?
Partner two	Yes.
The director	Are you openly and publicly agreeing to spend

many years with this person, knowing what they are like?

Partner two   I am.

The second partner now gives a copy of their own Book of Imperfections to the first partner and says:

I give you this book, in which I have recorded the serious and deep failings of my character – as well as I can understand them at the moment – but knowing there are sure to be others, which may be even worse. As a proof of love and trust, I'm showing you what I know to be terrible about me. These are the broken parts of myself, for which I need forgiveness. I am frightened of, and humbled by, the power this gives you. Yet I still want to marry you and hope you still want to marry me.

The director addresses the first partner, who has just received the book and asks: Do you understand the seriousness of what's written here?

Partner one   Yes.

The director   Have you read it carefully?

Partner one   Yes.

The director   Will you treat this knowledge with kindness?

Partner one   Yes, I will.

The director   Do you promise not to use this knowledge to embarrass your partner in front of other people?

Partner one	Yes.
The director	There may be more faults to come. Can you live with them?
Partner one	Yes.
The director	Are you openly and publicly agreeing to spend many years with this person, knowing what they are like?
Partner one	I am.

The director asks the couple to face each other (up till now they have been facing the congregation). Then the director asks the couple to recite to each other a short statement.

The couple say together:

Both partners	Neither of us is fully sane or healthy. We are committed to treating each other, as broken people, with enormous kindness and imagination – when we can manage it.

The director addresses the congregation:

The director	There is nothing odd about this couple beyond the ordinary oddness that is everyone's lot. They have merely put into words the errors and failings of which we are all continuously guilty.
The congregation	We are all broken.
	We have all been idiots and will be idiots again.

We are all difficult to live with: we sulk and get angry, blame others for things that are our own responsibility, have strange obsessions and fail to compromise.

We are here to try to make you less lonely with your failings. We will mostly never know the details. But we understand.

We understand.

These words can be set to music in a way that everyone will be able to join in. Collective singing is a very unusual experience for most people and therefore it can further heighten the emotional drama of the moment.

There now follows the first reading, which expands on the idea of humility and its constructive role in marriage.

SUGGESTED FIRST READING

The failings of our partners can be deeply galling. We look upon their faults and wonder why they are the way they are.

At moments of particularly acute agitation, we need to rehearse an idea called the Weakness of Strength. This dictates that we should always strive to see our partner's weaknesses as the inevitable downside of certain merits that drew us to them, and from which we will benefit at other points – even if none of these benefits are apparent at present. What we are seeing are not their faults, pure and simple, but rather the shadow side of things that are genuinely good about them. We're picking up on weaknesses that derive from strengths.

In the 1870s, when he was living in Paris, the American novelist Henry James became a good friend of the celebrated Russian novelist Ivan Turgenev, who was also living in the city at that time. Henry James was particularly taken by the unhurried, tranquil style of the Russian writer's storytelling. He obviously took a long time over every sentence, weighing different options, changing, polishing, until – at last – everything was perfect. It was an ambitious, inspiring approach to writing.

But in personal and social life, these same virtues could make Turgenev a maddening companion. He'd accept an invitation to lunch; then – the day before – send a note explaining that he would not be able to attend; then another saying how much he looked forward to the occasion. Then he would turn up – two hours late. Making arrangements with him was a nightmare. Yet his social waywardness was really just the same thing that made him so attractive as a writer. It was the same unwillingness to hurry; the same desire to keep the options open until the last moment. This produced marvellous books – and dinner party chaos. In reflecting on Turgenev's character, Henry James reflected that his Russian friend was exhibiting the 'weakness of his strength'.

Every strength that an individual possesses brings with it a weakness of which it is an inherent part. It is impossible to have strengths without weaknesses. Every virtue has an associated weakness. Not all the virtues can belong together in a single person.

This should subtly alter the way we see the defects and weakness of our partners. Our minds tend to hive off the strengths and see these as essential, while deeming the weaknesses freakish superfluities; in truth, the weaknesses are part and parcel of the strengths.

We must overcome the unhelpful idea that – if only we looked a little harder – we would find an unbroken soul. If strengths are invariably connected to failings, there won't be anyone who is remotely flawless. We may find people with different strengths, but they will also have a new litany of weaknesses. Human beings are not made for, and therefore should never aspire to, perfection.

To close the ritual, a short piece of music is played, which condenses the themes of humility. The mood is openly sorrowful and plaintive: something fragile, weak and easily damaged is being exposed; it's sorry and ashamed and not confident that it deserves to be forgiven. It's putting itself in the hands of another and asking for love.

THE RITUAL OF CHARITY

The director

In your life together, both of you will inevitably do many things that will upset and distress the other. It will be normal to be angry, to sulk, to be tempted to have an affair. You will condemn, you might gossip about the faults of the other; you will blame them for your sorrows; you will accuse them rather than take responsibility for yourself. When they act badly (as they will) you will often interpret them harshly; you will impute the worst motives to them.

The director invites the partners to repeat the following statements:

I will try not to malign you.

I will try not to have an affair.

I will try to understand what you attempt to communicate to me and not always merely pick up on the words you use, which may be meaner or more brusque than you intend.

I will try to explain my worries calmly and without accusations.

When I fail, I will try to admit my errors without turning on you.

The director continues:

Charity is at the heart of love. Charity means finding the least alarming, least panicked view of why the other is acting as they are. It sees the fear behind the aggression; it sees the loneliness at the root of a sulk; it recognises how shame can make a person defiant and how a hidden worry can unleash excessive harshness.

Will you now exchange the ritual gifts of charity?

Each partner exchanges a framed photograph of themselves as a child. The photographs are beautifully framed; they are important gifts.

The director explains to the congregation what is going on:

The couple are exchanging photographs of one another from childhood. We naturally act towards a child with a spirit of love that we often find it hard to adopt towards adults. This exchange of childhood images symbolises a commitment to treat one another with the kindness one wouldn't hesitate to show a child but so often refuse grown-ups.

Both partners together

I will place this child version of you at the centre of my love. I will try to see your faults as a consequence of troubles in your past. I will look after the broken child within you.

The congregation

When with a child, we feel charity.
We don't rush to blame.
We look for attenuating circumstances.
We're slow to anger.
We're quick to forgive.

Your partner was a child – and they are still somewhere the same person they once were.
When you shout, you are shouting at this child.
When you betray, you are betraying this child.
When you blame, you are blaming this child.
The photo urges patience, tolerance and warmth.

The director

We now hear the second reading.

SUGGESTED SECOND READING

At its most basic, charity means giving someone something they need but can't get for themselves. Normally this is understood to mean something material. We overwhelmingly associate charity with giving money. But, at its core, charity goes far beyond finance. It is about the interpretation of motives. It involves seeing that another person's bad behaviour is not a sign of wickedness or sin, but is a result of suffering. The psychologically charitable feel inwardly 'fortunate' enough to be able to come forward with explanations of others' misdeeds – their impatience or over-ambition, rashness or rage – that take attenuating circumstances into account. They generate a picture of who another person might be that can make them seem more than simply mean or mad. In financial matters, charity tends always to flow in one direction. The philanthropist may be very generous, but they normally stay rich; they are habitually the giver rather than the recipient. But in our relationships with others more broadly, the need for charity is unlikely ever to end up being one-sided, for we all stand in need of constant and shifting generosity of interpretation.

We are never far from requiring help in explaining to the world why we are not quite as awful as we seem.

Small children sometimes behave in stunningly unfair and shocking ways: they scream at the person who is looking after them, angrily push away a bowl of animal pasta, throw away something you have just fetched for them. But we rarely feel personally agitated or wounded by their behaviour. And the reason is that we don't assign a negative motive or mean intention to a small person. We reach around for the most benevolent interpretations. We don't think they are doing it in order to upset us. We probably think that they are a bit tired, or their gums are sore, or they are upset by the arrival of a younger sibling. We have a large repertoire of alternative explanations ready in our heads – and none of these lead us to panic or get terribly agitated.

This is the reverse of what tends to happen around adults in general, and our lovers in particular. Here we imagine that others deliberately have us in their sights. They probably relish the thought of causing us distress. But if we employed the infant model of interpretation, our first assumption would be quite different: maybe they didn't sleep well last night and are too exhausted to think straight; maybe they have a sore knee; maybe they are doing the equivalent of testing the boundaries of parental tolerance.

It's very touching that we live in a world where we have learnt to be so kind to children: now we must learn to be a little more generous towards the childlike parts of one another.

The ritual of charity closes with a short piece of music: the mood is oceanic, gentle, tender. It might have qualities in common with a lullaby.

THE RITUAL OF RE-ENCHANTMENT

The director

This couple has been drawn together because of what they admire and appreciate in one another. But it is normal that over time, under the pressure of daily life, their attractive and endearing qualities will grow obscure. They will forget the privilege of having been let into one another's lives. We acknowledge the risk head on, and attempt to avert it.

Both partners together

The good things about you will fade from my mind.

I will forget, under the pressure of our crowded calendars, the wondrousness of you.

We will be buried under administration, we will be preoccupied by points of disagreement.

At times, we'll see only what is wrong with someone we once cherished.

The director

The lovely, fascinating, sweet and impressive qualities that you have seen in one another will always continue to exist – even when they are lost from sight in times of stress, lassitude and rage.

I want to direct your attention to a part of you that it was once particularly tender to have the right to touch. Please take hold of one another's right hands.

The partners hold each other's right hands.

The director	This was the hand that, when you were initially granted permission to touch it, left you filled with excitement and wonder.
	It is the same hand. Its unique arrangement of lines and creases remains the same. The gaps between the fingers, the quirks of the veins and nails – these are places where an especially private kind of autobiography is inscribed.
	Look into each other's eyes. Vow to stay loyal to what a held hand symbolises: tenderness, mutual respect, appreciation.
	Repeat after me: I will vow to keep looking at this person with all the wonder they deserve.
Both partners together	I will vow to keep looking at this person with the wonder they deserve.
The director	I will try to see what I could see at the beginning.
Both partners together	I will try to see what I could see at the beginning.
The director	It was an unprecedented gift when they first let me hold this hand; it remains the same privilege today.
Both partners together	It was an unprecedented gift when they first let me hold this hand; it remains the same privilege today.
	There is silence for a few moments.
The director	It is time for a third and final reading.

SUGGESTED THIRD READING

After being together with someone for a few years, their attractions stand to become grievously familiar. We will ignore them and become experts on their most trying dimensions. But we are never without a chance to reverse the process. It might be that we watch them when they are with friends. We pick up again on their shy smile, their sympathetic look, or the purposeful way they push back the sleeves of their pullover. Or perhaps we hear that a casual acquaintance thinks that they are fascinating and elegant and – mixed in with a dose of jealous irritation – via this potential rival's eye, we see again all that we could conceivably lose.

We are adaptable creatures. Disenchantment is not a one-way street. We are capable of a second, more accurate look. We can turn to art for hints on how to perform the manoeuvre of re-enchantment. Many works of art look with particular focus at what has been ignored and taken for granted. In the 18th century, the French painter Chardin didn't paint the grand things that other painters of the period went in for: heroic battles, majestic landscapes or dramatic scenes from history. Instead he looked around him and portrayed the quiet, ordinary objects of everyday life: kitchen utensils, a basket of fruit, a teacup. He brought to these objects a deeply loving regard. Normally you might not have given them a moment's thought. But, encouraged by Chardin, we start to see their allure. He's not pretending; he's showing us their real but easily missed virtues. He isolates them, he concentrates attention, he carefully notes what is worthy of respect. He re-enchants our perception.

In the 19th century, the English painter John Constable did something similar for clouds. Nothing, perhaps, sounds duller. Maybe as children we liked to watch the grey banks of cloud drift and scud across the arc of the sky. We had favourites among them; we saw how they merged and separated; how they were layered; how a blue patch could be revealed and then swiftly covered. Clouds are lovely things, we once knew. Then we forgot. Constable's many cloud paintings remind us of the ethereal poetry unfolding above our heads at all moments, ready to delight us when we have the imagination to look up.

Also in the 19th century, the painter Claude Monet took his easel into the fields not far from Paris. Others from the city were heading off to exotic places to find beauty: to the fjords of Norway, to the temples of Egypt, to the Atlas Mountains or the plains of Patagonia. Monet re-found the beauty that was already there, to hand: poppies in a meadow, sunlight on stone, a pond in a suburban garden, a train pulling into a busy railway station. They were not exotic things: they are things we could (and do) grow bored of – until, helped by Monet – we are re-sensitised to their grace and dignity.

Imagine meeting your partner through the lens of art. You would find again the allure of things about them that – through familiarity and haste – had been neglected. We could study once more the magic of a palm that we once longed to caress;

we could attend again to a way of tilting the head that once seemed so suggestive. In the early days, we knew how to see. Now as artists of our lives – in our own fashion – we can rediscover, we can select, refocus, appreciate. We can become the explorers of lost continents filled with one another's overlooked qualities.

There now follows a short piece of music. The mood is of joyful surprise, perhaps starting in a more sombre way before the feeling lightens and clears.

THE EXCHANGE OF RINGS AND THE SPOUSAL VOW

The director invites the congregation to stand.

The director

Knowing all this, fearing all this, hoping all this, will you, in front of all of us, vow to wed each other? Will you agree to share your lives – with all the restraint and sorrow that will be involved, as well as the joy, the kindness and the friendship?

The director turns to the first partner and says: At this moment, time is suspended; you are speaking now for all the times of your life. Are you willing to marry ... ?

Partner one

I am.

The director

The director turns to the second partner and says: At this moment, time is suspended; you are speaking now for all the times of your life. Are you willing to marry ... ?

Partner two

I am.

The director

I invite ... and ... to exchange rings, symbols of mutual commitment, and proof of a willingness to limit their freedom for the greater freedom of love and of a vow to merge their joys and sorrows.

An exchange of rings.

I now declare you married.

The couple kiss; it should be a solemn gesture.

After a pause of a few moments, the director signals to the congregation to say the following together:

The congregation

We have heard your vows.
We hope for you.
We fear for you.
We see in your hopes our own hopes.
We see in your fears our own fears.
We won't be there in the darkness of night,
But think of us when it feels impossible.
We know.
We understand.
We have been in our own night.
You won't see us all here again.
But keep our spirit alive in your memories.
Our marriages were
Or are
Or will be
Very far from perfect.
But we can learn and recover and improve.
May your wisdom increase.
May this marriage be enough.
With all our hearts we wish you the best.

There is a musical option for these words, designed for everyone to join in and to heighten further the mood of fellowship in the face of the tasks of marriage.

The couple step down from the platform and walk out slowly, while a final piece of music is played. The closing music should be triumphant. The mood is one of confidence and joy. It speaks of obstacles overcome, pain transcended: spring after winter.

THE FUNERAL

For religions, dying was regarded as an essential, immensely important, part of existence; it was supposed to happen at a time appointed by God or by fate. It was not an embarrassing or despair-inducing end point, it was a transformation: the soul would continue its life in another form or in another place. Those who died had only 'departed' and lived on elsewhere. Perhaps after our own death, our souls would be reunited with theirs.

By contrast, in modernity, death cannot help but come across as an insult. It is a fundamental rebuke to meritocracy, progress, technology and to individualism; it is a failure of independence. Modernity has prolonged our lives but it has also taken away the consolations that religion used to offer at their inevitable terminations.

Religions developed impressive and solemn funeral rituals to stress the dignified character of death. We can end up with a yearning for some of what they offered even when we don't share the underlying beliefs that animated their ceremonies.

We imagine a funeral service filled with a sequence of consolations – delivered by a Director.

THE SURREAL NATURE OF DEATH

The director

Death is at once the strangest and most normal thing that can happen in a life. A beloved of infinitely complex consciousness no longer exists; atoms arranged in an inexorably unique sequence are now forever dispersed. The moment seems like a rebuke to everything we are and hope for; it is contrary to all the stability and continuity we crave – but it was preordained from the moment of birth. Nothing fundamentally heinous has happened. There was never going to be another way – and they knew it, as we do. The death feels so wrong, but death is written into the contract of existence. What has happened is an outrage and at the same time the fulfilment of a basic pledge we all undertake at the moment of our birth. It is life, not death, that is the anomaly. Death is our one great common destiny, the event from which all our love and compassion flows. We will miss them so much.

THE LEGITIMACY OF GRIEF

The director

We are, and will be going forward, under subtle pressure to get over what has happened. It will be suggested that we move on, that we put things in perspective, that we understand what had to be.

There is no need for any of this. We will never 'get over' our loss in any simple way. We won't ever forget or naively 'recover' – and we don't have to. Our ongoing grief is simply the price we pay for having loved. One day, very far from now, the memory of what has happened will still be capable of striking us with its full devastating force, as if we had only just received the news. We won't ever be able to put it behind us conclusively – and shouldn't expect to. Death is not something we should ever rightly want to overcome. Love is, in this sense, eternal. Mourning does not need to have an endpoint. We can bear that this loss will never leave us. We miss them so much.

The director asks the congregation to say together:

The congregation

We need never stop missing them,
Because we need never stop loving them.
Grief is the price we pay for love.

GRATITUDE

The director

They would be touched that we have gathered
here for them. They would be moved by the efforts
we have made – and by our tears. They would
be saddened by our sadness. They would seek
to comfort us for the agony of no longer having
them in our lives. They would want us to miss
them – and at the same time, they would hope for
their memory not simply to be a source of pain.
They would seek for us to remember that behind,
and prior to, this pain, there was joy, tenderness,
fascination, insight, loyalty and moments of sheer
fun. They would want us to endure. They would
not want us to feel that we could not survive
without them, though they would be so touched by
the present conviction that we can't.

AMBIVALENCE

The director

We can feel an acute pressure to speak well of
the dead; we want, above all, to express our love
and respect. But we can admit without guilt
that the dead are no different from the living:
they were as we are, beautifully flawed and
fascinatingly complicated. Our relationship to
them had ambiguous sides. Of course it did.
There were frustrations and disappointments;

misunderstandings that couldn't be put right;
resentments and anxieties and tantalising hopes
that were never quite fulfilled. Our relationship to
them was like this, because this is the nature of
all human loves. It's not a denial of love because
love involves closeness and closeness is necessarily
intricate. Love reaches out to encompass the
whole of someone's being and the whole is of
indescribable multiplicity. Because we love, we
understand the difficult forces at work inside
them. Ambivalence isn't a refusal of love, it is
a consequence of the profoundest kind of love.
Love doesn't involve saying someone is perfect; it
involves deploying deep and ongoing imagination
and generosity in trying to understand them.

REGRETS

The director

We may feel we didn't always love them as we
now wish we had. There were things we didn't
do, or things we wish we hadn't done; things we'd
change, if only we could.

We do not have to worry. We treated them as living
beings, and this is what they wanted and expected.
Most of what we wanted to say made its way to
them indirectly. We didn't have to put it explicitly
into words. They knew or guessed. They didn't
say everything either. It's how human relations
function: we do not have to spell everything out,
because we do so much of the work in our own
minds. They knew enough that we cared and why,
at points, there were difficulties. They understood
that there was sufficient love; it's why we're here
now; they wouldn't be surprised to see us. They
would know why we had come.

IMMORTALITY

The director

The moment when someone dies is not when their body ceases to exist, but when the last person whose life was touched by them dies. On this basis, they have so long left to live. They continue to survive within us. The conversation with them goes on without end in our own minds. They will be us through things that have not yet happened, through so many dilemmas, joys and sorrows to come. We will take them into our confidences. We will hear their voice completely and clearly and they will advise and console us. Death cannot rob us of this. They live within us now.

AT PEACE

The director

Our love can do strange things. It can produce fears that the one we've lost might be feeling abandoned, might be in pain somewhere, might be feeling alone and dejected; that we are currently letting them down or failing to look after them. We mustn't worry. They are not unhappy. They are properly at peace. They don't need us now. They don't blame us for anything. They are not angry with us. We cannot hurt or disappoint them. They do not resent us for being alive. It may be frightening to die; it is not frightening to be dead. They are at peace.

The director asks the congregation to say together:

The congregation

They are not unhappy
They do not need us
Though we still need them;
We miss them so much.

ENDURANCE

The director

We will never forget them, but we will live, tomorrow and the next day. This is not ingratitude or callousness. It is loyalty to the values we shared with them. We can live on and still be faithful to everything they meant for us. It's not an attack on love to endure and to love again. Love wants what's good for the other; love wants there to be more love. They will accompany us as we leave this place today – and they will follow us through the rest of our lives. No one can separate us from them.

We miss them so much – and yet they are still here.

XI.

CONCLUSION

✳

This book has been filled with ideas about to how to replace the rituals and practices of religions.

The exercise was not meant to be conclusive. There might be many more concepts that could fruitfully be highlighted and given prominence in secular societies. We are – above anything else – trying to kick-start a process of reflection and, eventually, action.

Our real mission is to highlight the number of areas where we at present have gaps left by the evaporation of religion from our lives, and to suggest some ways in which our organisation, and many others, could start to locate and instill adequate replacements.

CREDITS

p.8
The Round Reading Room,
The British Museum, c.2001.
© The Trustees of the British
Museum.

p.9
Rijksmuseum underpass,
2016. Photograph © Peter
Heeling / Skitterphoto.

p.12
Charles Henry Granger,
Auguste Comte, France,
1798-1857.

p.13
Positivist Temple in Porto
Alegre, Brazil, 2007.
Tetraktys /Wikimedia
Commons.

p.14
Louis-Jules Etex, *Clotilde
de Vaux*, c.1798-1857 / Jean
Pierre Dalbéra

p.45
Chartres Cathedral,
France, 1220.
© John Kellerman / Alamy
Stock Photo.

p.48
Johannes Vermeer, *The
Milkmaid*, c.1657–1658.
Purchased with the support of
the Vereniging Rembrandt.

p.49
Johannes Vermeer,
The Little Street, c.1657–1658.
Gift of H.W.A. Deterding,
London.

p.73
(top)
Sheikh Lotfollah Mosque,
Iran, 2009,
by Mostafa Meraji licensed
under CC BY-SA 4.0.

(bottom)
Rozan-ji - Kyoto (Japan) 2019.
© White Images / Scala,
Florence.

p.76
(top)
St Michael's Church,
Bavaria, c. 1583–1597.
© ImageBROKER / Alamy
Stock Photo.

(bottom)
Urnes Stave Church,

Norway, c. 1130.
© Jan Wlodarczyk / Alamy
Stock Photo

p.81
Temple to Perspective, 2010
© Tom Greenall & Jordan
Hodgson.

p.85
Sandro Botticelli,
*Lamentation over the Dead
Christ*, c.1490.

p.87
(left)
Seated Buddha, Thailand, 15th
century. Gift of Mr. and Mrs.
A. Richard Benedek, 1981.

(right)
Buddha, Sri Lanka, 18th
century.
Purchase, Louis V. Bell,
Harris Brisbane Dick,
Fletcher, and Rogers Funds
and Joseph Pulitzer Bequest;
The Miriam and Ira D.
Wallach Foundation Fund;
Florence and Herbert Irving,
Cynthia Hazen Polsky and
Anne H. Bass Gifts, 2010.

p.88
(top)
Tintoretto, *Christ Washing the
Disciples' Feet*, 1549.

(bottom)
Ford Madox Brown,
Jesus Washing Peter's Feet,
1856.

p.109
The Golden Temple, Kyoto,
1397, by Jaycangel licensed
under CC BY-SA 3.0.

p.114
Confessional in a Catholic
church, a Romanesque church
detail inside. sergiobarrios ©
123RF.com

p.119
Fra Angelico, *The Forerunners
of Christ with Saints and
Martyrs*. 1424.
© Alamy / Fine Art Images /
Heritage Images.

The School of Life is a global organisation helping people lead more fulfilled lives. It is a resource for helping us understand ourselves, for improving our relationships, our careers and our social lives – as well as for helping us find calm and get more out of our leisure hours. We do this through films, workshops, books, gifts and community. You can find us online, in stores and in welcoming spaces around the globe.